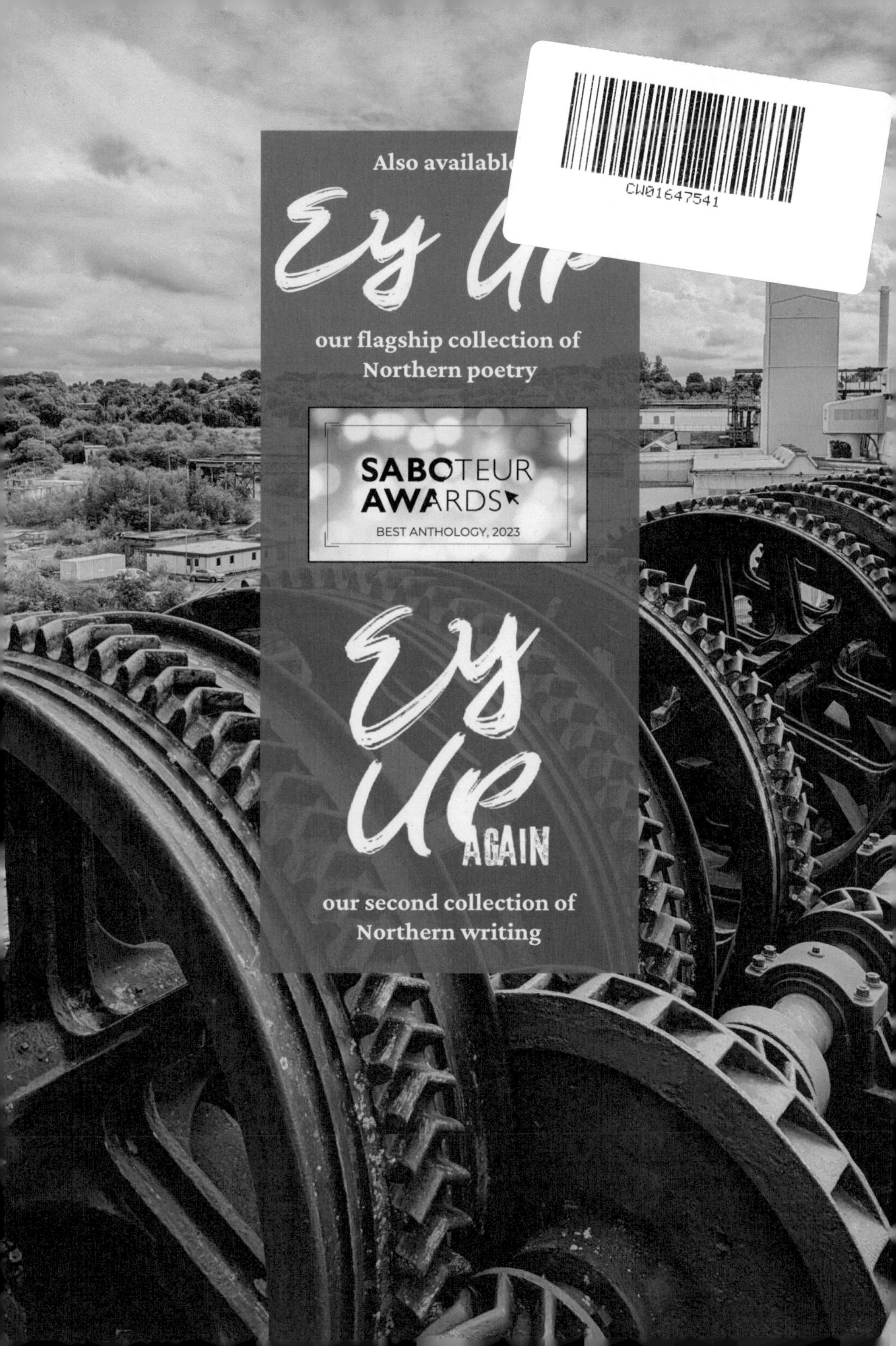
Also available
Ey Up
our flagship collection of Northern poetry
SABOTEUR AWARDS
BEST ANTHOLOGY, 2023
Ey Up AGAIN
our second collection of Northern writing

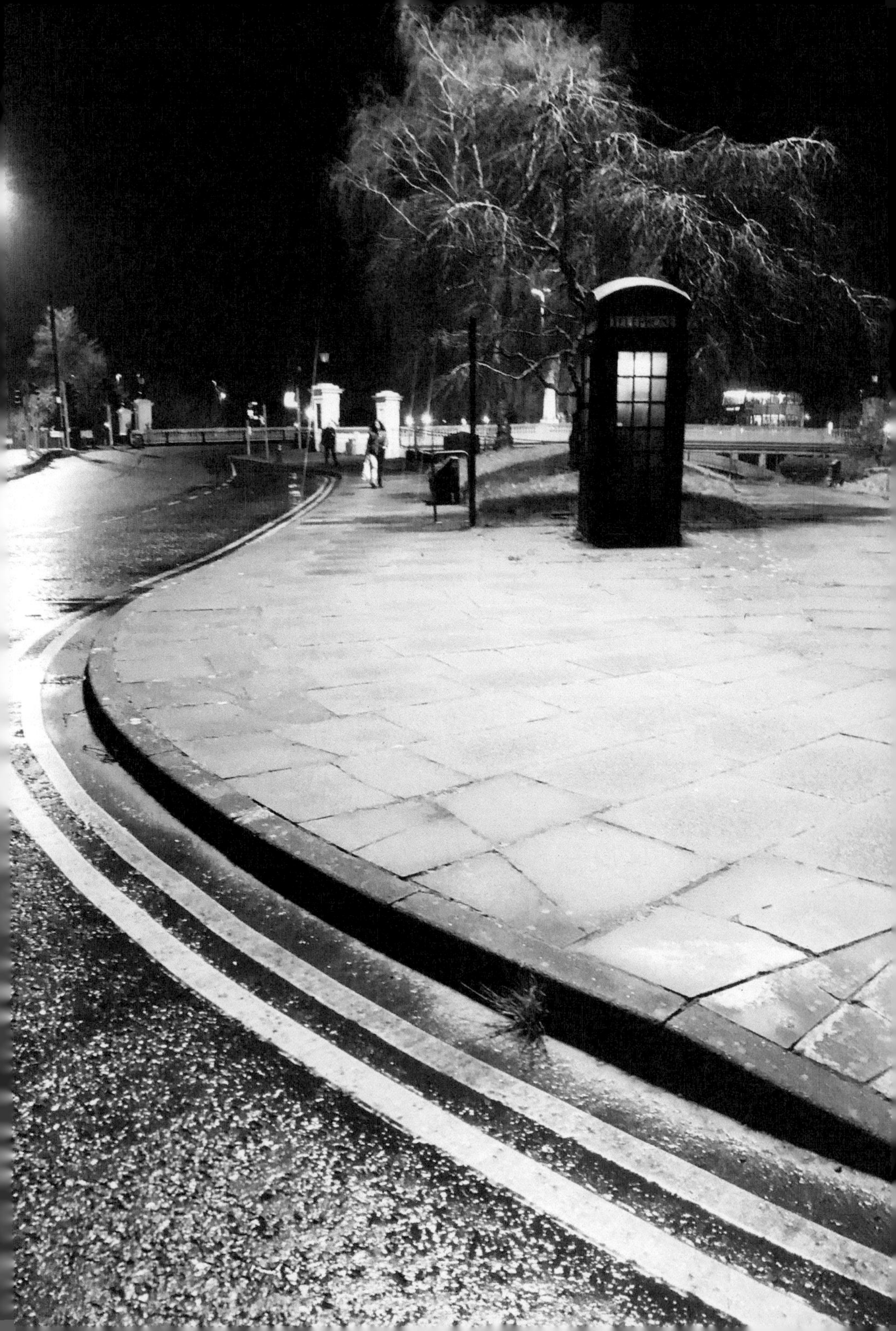

Ey Up 3

An Anthology of Northern Writing and Photography

Edited by
Alex Callaghan

written off publishing

First published in Great Britain by Written Off Publishing™, 2024

ISBN: 978-1-915320-44-5

Written Off Publishing
Owley Wood Road, Weaverham
www.writtenoffpublishing.com

Collated and edited by Alex Callaghan @ Written Off
Cover art © Sophie Rose

Printed in the UK on recycled paper by Mixam UK Ltd using vegetable-based inks.

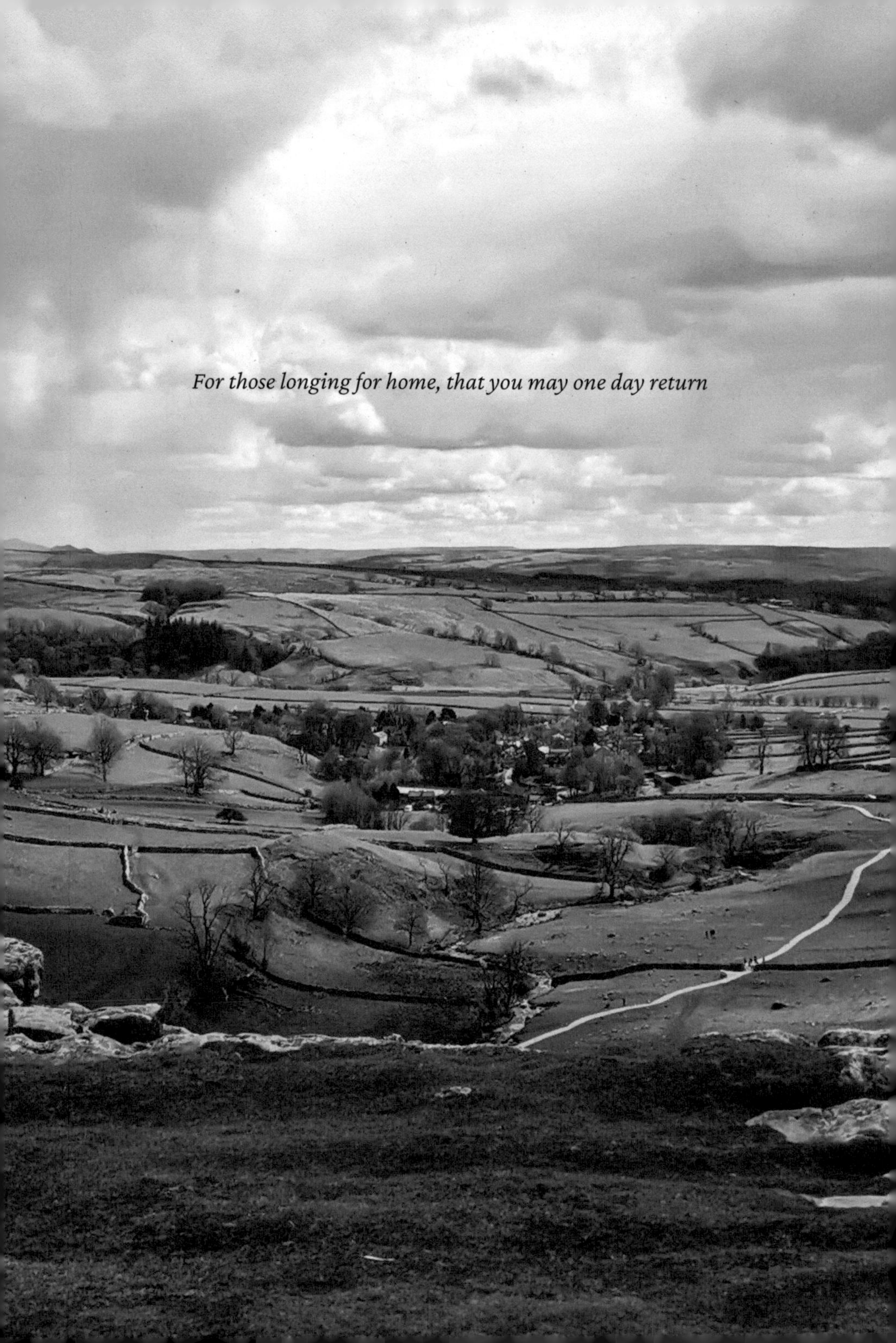

For those longing for home, that you may one day return

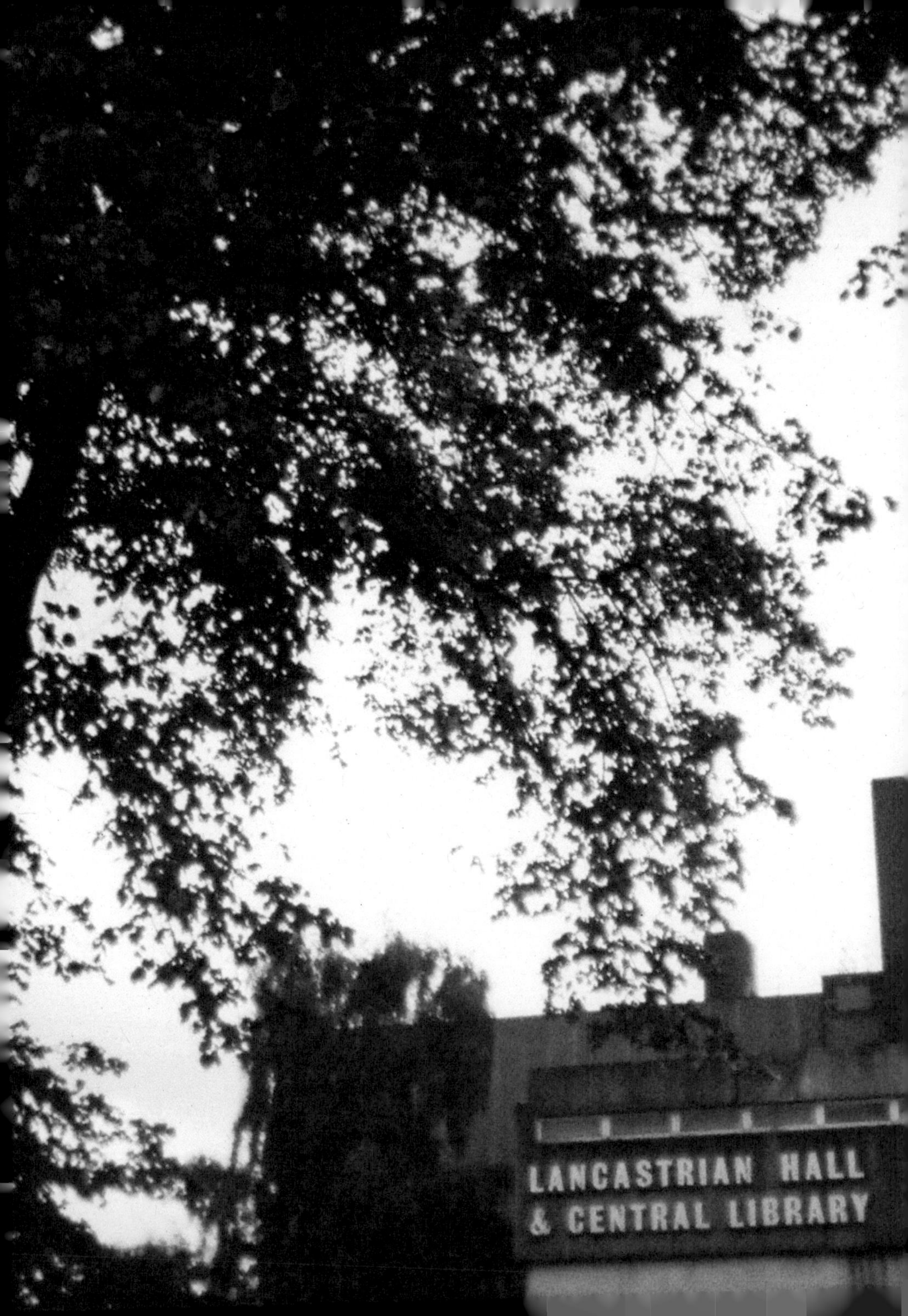
LANCASTRIAN HALL
& CENTRAL LIBRARY

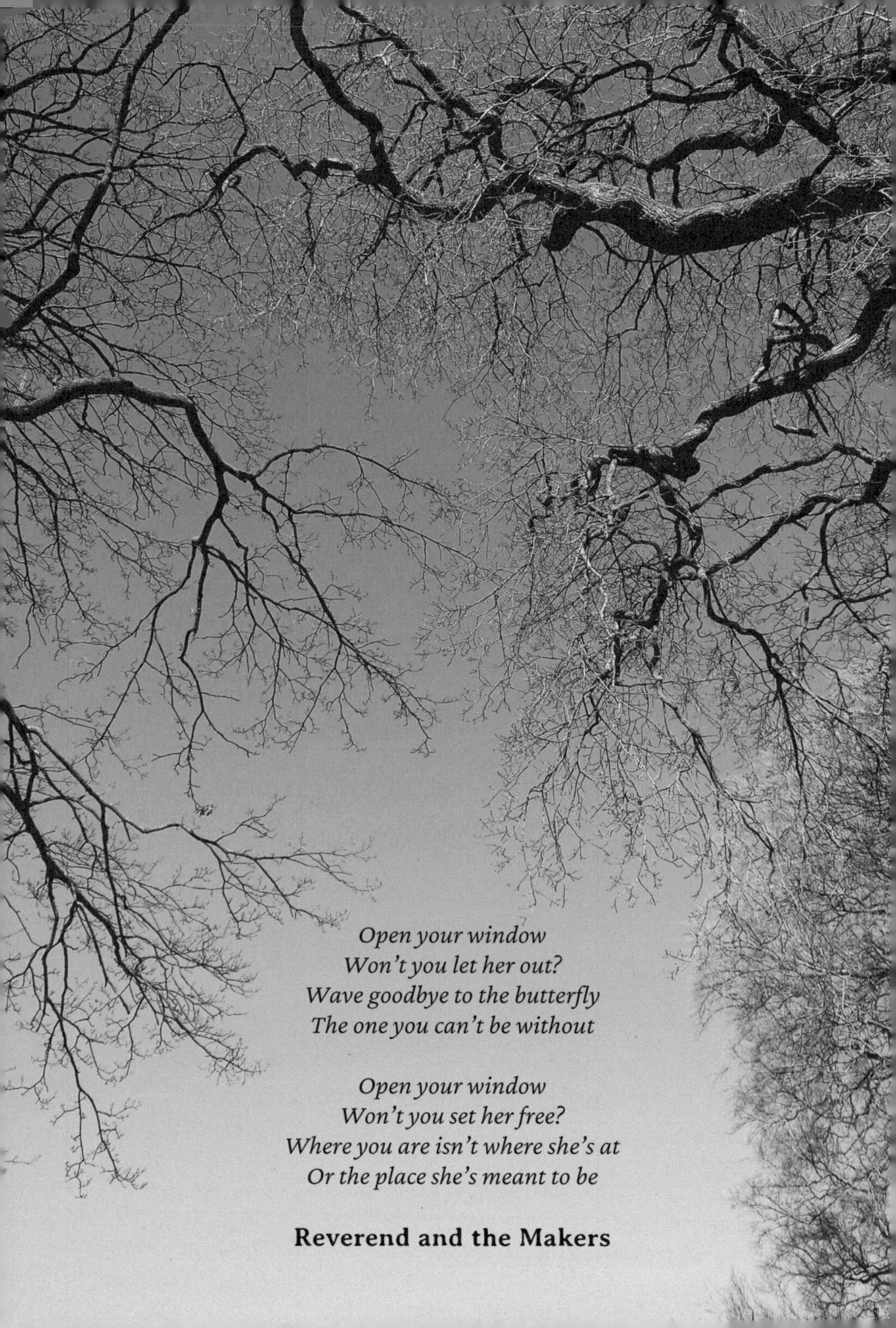

Open your window
Won't you let her out?
Wave goodbye to the butterfly
The one you can't be without

Open your window
Won't you set her free?
Where you are isn't where she's at
Or the place she's meant to be

Reverend and the Makers

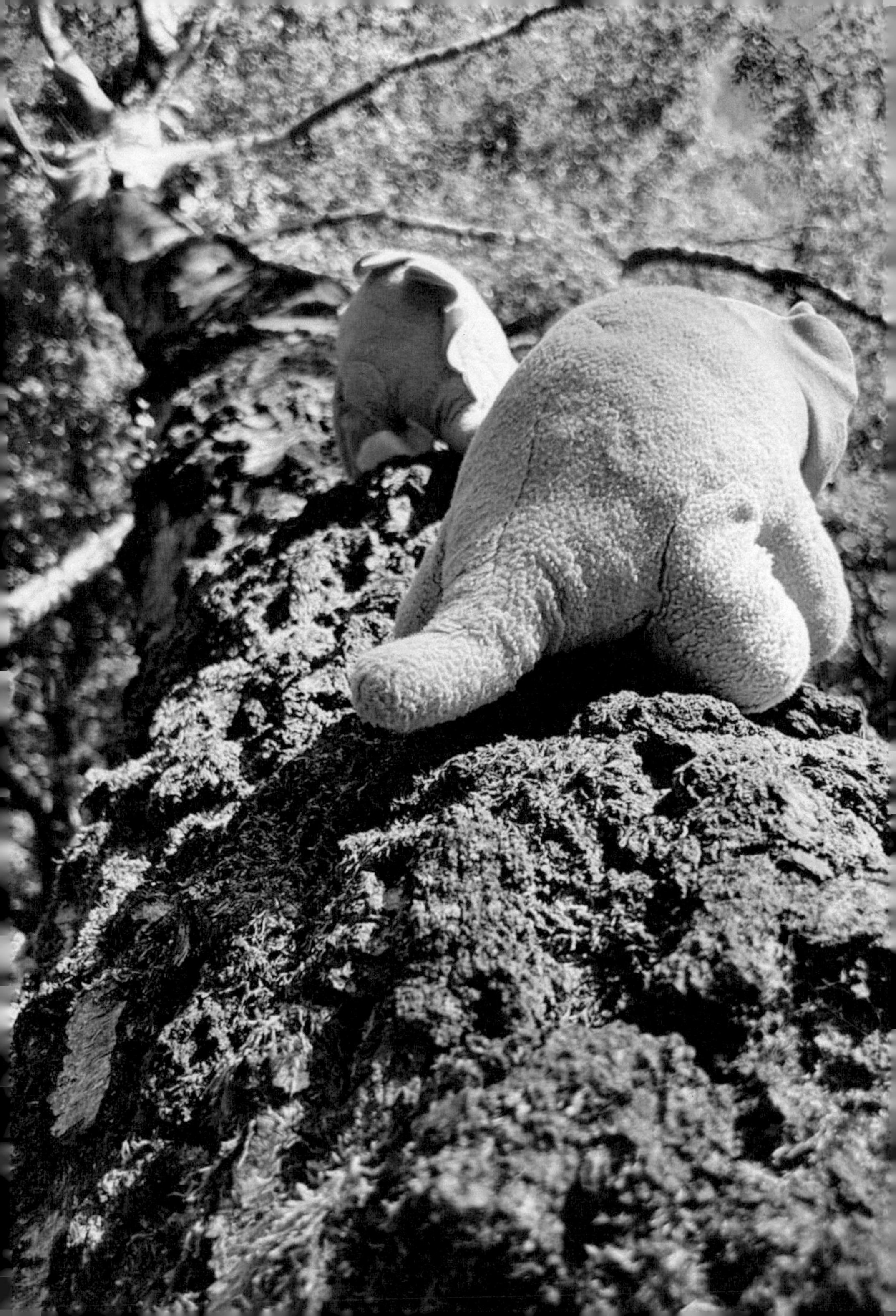

Contents

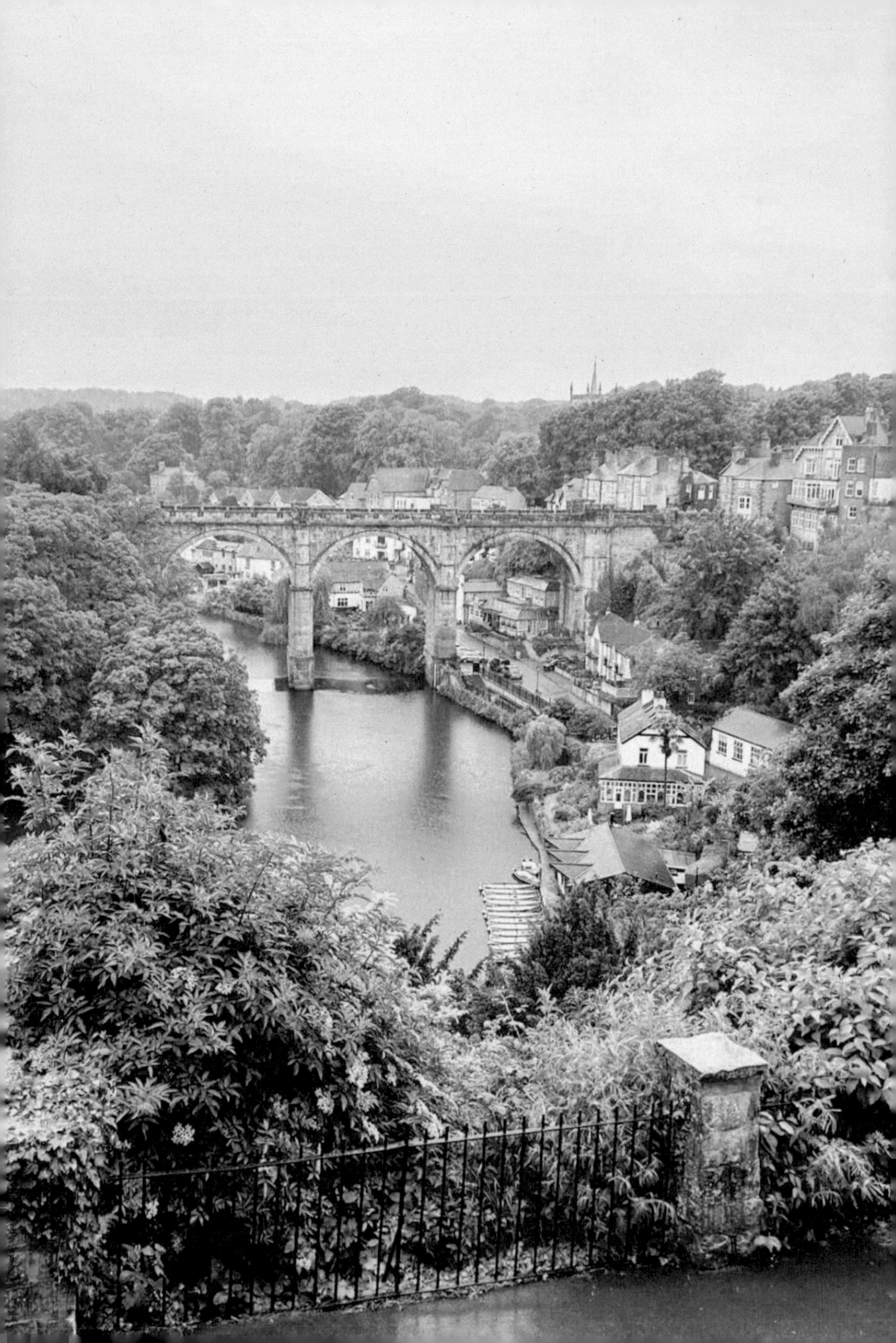

Foreword

Pride is etched into the landscape of the North, echoing down from steep hills to winding valleys, getting lost on the sea air, and swearing at strangers from across the street.

The third instalment of Written Off Publishing's award winning Northern anthology, Ey Up 3 is a celebration of the many complexities of the North of England in the voices of those who call it home. Through poetry and prose, this anthology is a life cycle: starting at birth, pummeling though a world that never stops, following Northerners who dare to wonder – to love, to leave, to lose; to rediscover what home is and to long for it in all weathers (and as we all know, the weather is often foul).

The people in this book are brave. They are sharing their words with you – some of them for the very first time. Not only their words and their dialect, but also their past and present, their loved ones, their hopes and fears. This is a collection of people's lives: the North as an ever changing landscape both shaped by, and shaping, its people.

The ever-changing landscape has been keenly felt this year by the felling of the Sycamore Gap tree, an event that has sparked plenty of commemorative art feeling its loss, including our cover art by the always excellent Sophie Rose, a fitting tribute in an anthology all about adapting to change.

The first Ey Up poetry anthology won a Saboteur Award for Best Anthology 2023. This was followed by Ey Up Again, which expanded submissions to include prose and arrived double the size of its predecessor. The community and support surrounding the Ey Up series of anthologies has been incredibly heartwarming, and as they say: three's company; three is a magic number; three's enough to third-wheel on a chess match.

For all of the above reasons, being trusted to edit Ey Up 3 has been a privilege. People's writing being in my care, and the support from

Rebecca and the team has meant the world to me. Despite all the evidence, it's easy to forget that I am good at this writing thing. If my younger self could see this, I think they'd be pretty freaked out by seeing a vision of the future, which might mess them up in the head for life and lead me to never edit this in the first place. It could also just be passed off as a strange dream, but as we'll never know which, it's probably best I get this bit over with and you get on with reading this excellent book.

So, is your kettle boiled? Is your seat comfortable? Then turn over the page and tuck right in.

Alex Callaghan
Editor

Ey Up 3

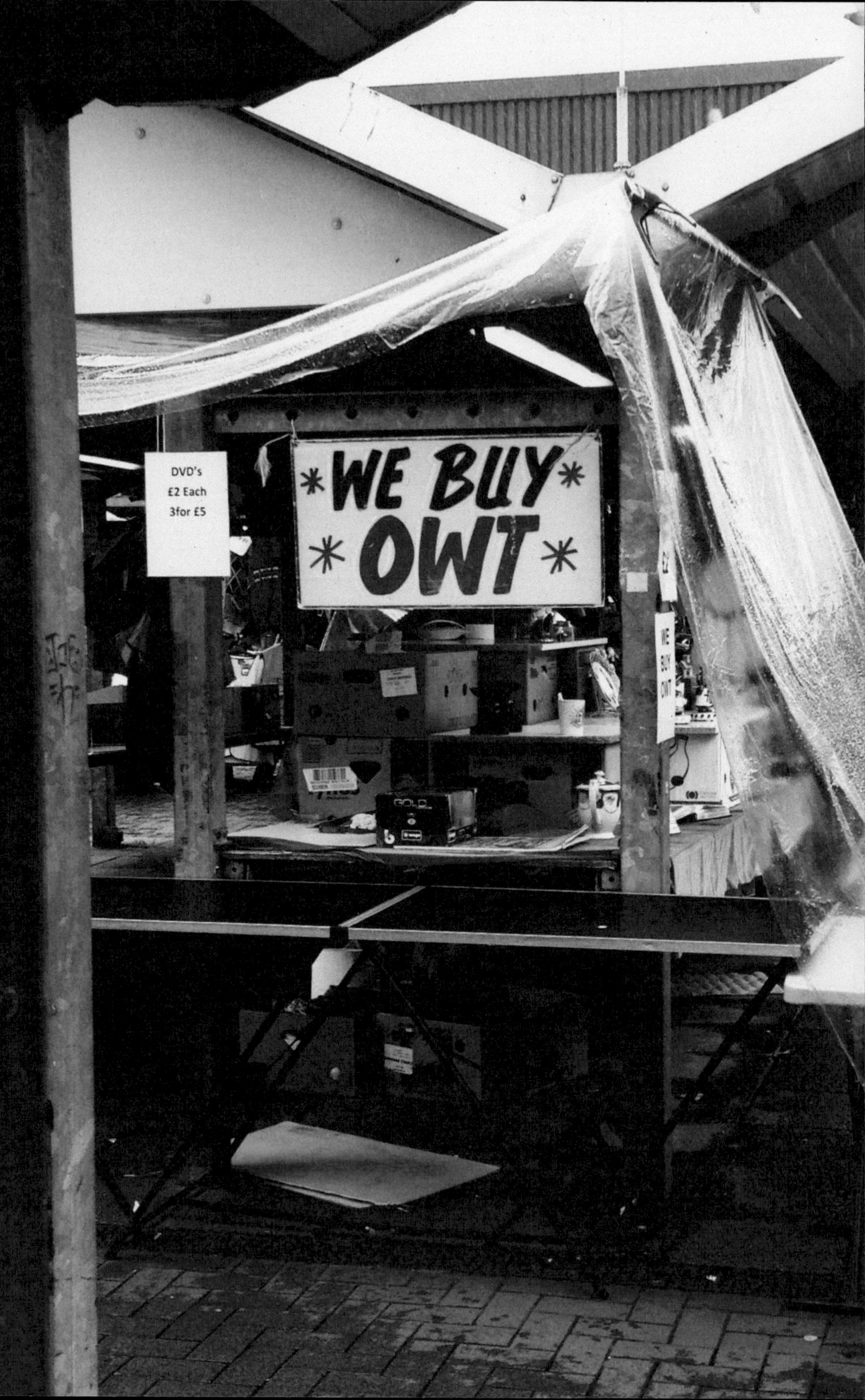
DVD's
£2 Each
3for £5
WE BUY
OWT
WE BUY OWT

The Näcken's Secret Name

One person saw what happened
but by the time the girl's body
had been dredged from the shallow water –
grey stones where her pretty eyes had been –
the entire village knew the story.

They didn't need to see the mud
caked under her nails, the rounds of grit
embedded in her grazed pink feet to know
that she'd been walking through the wood
when she'd heard the violin.

She'd have thought it was a bird at first.
A starling, maybe, imitating a song
that had drifted through the open window
of a house. She'd have followed it, enchanted,
until she'd found the player by the lake,

his fingers five bright birds bobbing on the strings.
When he'd stopped, she'd been unable to move
and he'd offered her a bargain: guess his name
or she would never see home again.
Erik? she guessed. *Magnus. Ragnar. Arne.*

With each wrong answer her feet moved
closer, closer to the water of their own accord.
The person who saw it wanted to help,
they truly did, but they'd had to block their ears
to stop the sound of their secret name.

[The Nordic näcken are male water spirits who play enchanted songs on the violin, luring women and children to drown in lakes or streams.]

Susan Darlington

My baby ate my brain

My baby ate my brain,
I'm not sure what remains,
He sucked my intellect out through my tit
Drained my energy, every. Last. Bit!
He feasted on my raw love
From the outside in,
Family watching from the side-lines
Willing the invasion to begin,
He devoured my soul and left a hole,
Gaping, vacuous, incapable of adult conversation,
Sleep, tea, fresh pyjamas — my only motivation,
I shuffle through the days
In a milk-stained, sick-reigned, sleep-deprived haze
But as I bask in the wonder of the miracle I made
I understand now the price of this maternal trade:
Babies get our brains
And motherhood is the regurgitated remains.

Esta Innes-Limbachia

Child

in our time, a boy walks the earth
born with twisted intestines
poison in his blood
and a decree of bruises for a birth certificate.
his skin still buzzes with the sting.
he struggles to see the sunlight
in the dandelion-freckled soil –
the begonias' amaranthine shades
only bloom on the edge of a knife.
the hymns in the birdsong drown in the screaming wind
and he can't fathom all the ways a river could make a wave.
still –
he walks a quiet pace
with a gentle touch never taught to him.
falls into step with the ants,
finds wayward moths in lampshades and sends them back toward the moon,
stretches a shaking hand to pet wild horses
and scours the fields for clovers
to hold in his palms until they wilt.

Ezekiel Foster-Eardley

Saturday Afternoons in the Late 90s

Sat cross-legged, cross-armed
Squished next to each other on the sofa.
Silenced with empty threats
And icy glares
As the TV repeats in its monotone type
The results and the scores...
EVERTON — NIL — SWANSEA — NIL
MANCHESTER UNITED — 5 — LIVERPOOL — 2

Forced to sit in silence for laughing too loud
For playing too rough
And for being four, five and seven
As he doesn't know what else to do.
And with a shove of an elbow and an 'ow'
Comes, 'WILL YOU THREE JUST SHUT UP?'
As the TV drones on
CHELSEA — NIL — WEST BROMWICH ALBION — 4

Nudges and whispers for fear of his growl
I'm thirsty, I need the toilet,
You ask him — no, you — I did it last time
Until he threw the icy stare, and silence, again
More shoving, more pushing
But gentle somehow
The silence only broken with the score
TOTTENHAM HOTSPUR — 4 — MIDDLESBROUGH — 2

Three sets of eyes sit and watch the clock
The minutes tick by like hours until ten past four
The back door opens with a tired sigh
As Mother heaves herself through the door
And throws herself into making tea
While the two younger ones make a fuss about her feet
And the eldest lingers by the door
ARSENAL — 2 — WEST HAM — 2

He doesn't notice her stand there
Eyes fixed on the screen, waiting for one result
The only one that matters
NEWCASTLE UNITED — NIL — SUNDERLAND — 1
And he explodes with emotion and anger
And throws something across the room
As his daughter turns her back on him again
To the sound of CRYSTAL PALACE — 1 — STOKE — NIL

Angela Marshall

Catherine Kilter

Catherine Kilter was a spoiled brat
an only child
her bedroom looked like the entire toy section
of the Argos catalogue
a doll's house so fancy
that I felt ashamed
going back home to our tiny council house
See on rainy days
she would give one of her friends
the great privilege
of entering her spotless house to play
Shoes off
Sunday manners
Thank you, Mrs Kilter,
Yes, I've washed my hands
No, I don't have nits this week
Dad used to say Mrs Kilter was
all fur coat and no knickers
Mum called her Mrs Hoity Toity
Catherine was just like her mother
dark-haired and pretty
with a cruel streak
that ran the length
of her upturned nose
Catherine had the ability
to make you feel as small
as one of her dolls

a room full of things to play with
yet her favourite game was peekaboo
hiding behind the curtains
laughing at the other kids
the ones that didn't make the grade that day
She'd make you play along
that was the sick payback for being chosen
while an uncomfortable feeling
growled in your stomach
knowing tomorrow
you would be
that rain-soaked peasant
Looking up enviously at the Princess
in her ivory tower

Linda Downs

Addicted to Shoes

Shoes all shapes
And sizes
Call out your name
Stilettos, sling-backs
Fatties and boots
Shoes for all seasons
Multiple use

Sat in shop windows
How long to remain
Price does not matter
When you pass again

Smell of new leather
Entice you to buy
Shoes have your name on
Go in and try!

Resisting temptation?
Not easy
That's true
Shoes in shop
Windows
Oh, what
Will you do

Tim Fletcher

Shatterproof

Miss hands us the three ruler sets — ruler, rubber, sharpener. One yellow, one red, one blue. Well done girls, excellent project. Soon as Miss' back is turned, Beccy grabs the red one. *This one is mine because my parents are socialists; you can 'ave the blue one.* She tosses it to me with mean, mascarared eyes. Why do I 'ave to 'ave the blue one? *What did yer dad say when you asked him ar'ee voted?* 'E said what guz on between a man n 'is ballot paper is secret business and that men fought and died ferrit. *Yeh, well me mum says that's what Tories always say so you can have the blue one. 'Er parents* — she jerks her thumb in Jane's direction — *'er mum's a teacher and 'er dad 'as a beard n rides a bike t'work, so she can 'ave the yella one.* Maybe Miss gev uz one of each colour cuz of ah teams? Jane says quietly.

I'm on the Blue team. Beccy's on the Red team. Jane's on the Yellow team. We've spent every Wednesday in May doing a group project on the building on the Channel Tunnel. The ruler sets are our reward for best project in class. We should have had someone from Green as well but we got Paula. Paula had first Wednesday off because her big sister lost a baby down the toilet and Paula wanted to look at it. Then she were off the next Wednesday because it was a week since the baby had been flushed and they were having a memorial service around her mum's dwarf conifer. Then she'd missed too much so we didn't want her back in our team and she's had to read in the corner on her own. She's not talking to us yet.

Anyway, I'm 'aving the red one. Liberals are just yella Tories anyway. Oo's coming wimme t'bench? We follow Beccy to the bench.

On the way home, down the jitty, when the other two have carried on down the street, I smash the ruler against the fence and watch it splinter. I dig my thumb nails into the rubber and split it into countless mini rubber balls. I stamp on the plastic sharpener and watch blue plastic mash with sun-softened tarmac.

Next morning, guilt greets me and I am late meeting the other two at the shops because I have stopped to stash all the bits in my bag.

I tell Miss I've got earache and she says I can stay in at break so long as she can have a fag out the Fire Exit as usual. She is gazing at the tennis courts while I empty my bag out on my desk. Spread all the bits of ruler over my workbook. Most of it is there but some pieces are missing.

Miss stubs her butt against the 'no entry' sign, slips back into her slingbacks and sighs back to her big desk. I tip the bits into my bag again and there they stay until the end of term.

Helen Rice

Meat & Potatoes

Dinner lady slops a heap
of mash and unnamed meat

onto my flimsy plastic plate.
It smells like bone marrow,

disinfectant and cat piss.
I want to tell her I don't like meat,

but the words turn fuzzy,
sticking on my teeth.

Instead, I follow the stream of kids
to the 'vegetable' section,

unsure whether to select anaemic carrots,
or peas in dishwater.

I opt for the latter –
at least they're still vaguely green.

Last stop is the bath of gravy,
I ladle it on by the gallon,

ignoring the lumps and chunks
of butter and mammal fat.

Cover anything in gravy
and the British think it a meal.

Subservience has gotten me this far,
until I take a bite, chew sinew, and vomit.

Alice Eaves

Owt or Nowt

Mrs Wisener won't permit owt or nowt
to enter the playground, says that
they're not words despite the fact
that Nana Amy uses them, and she's ninety-seven
so might have more knowledge than
someone who wears moth-eaten curtains.
I am persistent. I begin to use owt everywhere,
sprinkle it on my cereal in the morning,
stir it into tea, add owt to boiling water
and inhale the steam. I sing nowt in the shower,
dry myself on a vowel, scrawl it in the waistband
of my underwear. I order owt from restaurants,
nowt from drive-throughs, and sample the odd
owt milk latte. I wear nowt as a badge of an honour,
because Mrs Wisener calls it common and
I have always been stubborn. When told that
I can't use the words, I ignore anything and nothing
until all that I know is owt or nowt.

Charles Healthcote

Words of Affection

These words aren't mine:
they sit awkwardly in my mouth.
Those dropped consonants and round vowels never quite sound
how they should.
But nevertheless,
they're filled with love.

Scran, gan, pet lamb:
the words that created I am what I am,
the words from my gran that yawned with love over my body,
the words that solidly build my existence.
The *petal, hinnie* and *tuppence*
that were words which signified *hyem*.

And now *howay man* stumbles from my throat in a way that people
find awkward but helps me find home.
The reply of *aye* is a rallying cry that rumbled from my granda's
throat and twined round mine.

My lips, my tongue, my palate;
they didn't wait for the training we missed on how to fit in:
my larynx, my trachea, my epiglottis that
thought this was natural for us,
and still does,
aren't quite cut out for the Northern vowels but howl all the same
in unison for home.

Em MacKellar

Wildflowers on Manor

They grow where I grew up.
Fields by the council estate,
Where we'd play out.
Wild kids, untamed, dirty fingernails,
Sun-tanned noses.
Not planted intentionally,
Not wanted, you could say.
But you see the beauty in them anyway
Maybe you see yourself in them too.

You'd pick them for your mum,
And she'd lovingly take them
Place them in a pint glass of water
Probably stolen from the local.
Definitely stolen.
A universal sign of love, a wildflower
Picked by a wild little hand.

Natalie Hurt

University is not fer folk round 'ere

Nan and Grandad's woodchipped living room is yellow from years of soaking up Benson and Hedges. The comforting sweetness of tobacco clings to every cushion. I curl up surrounded by Nan's shiny brass trinkets, an umbrella of spider plants. I've found a spot where I'm not *in't road*, laid flat by the side of her armchair, on their red medallion carpet, running fingers over the plaited gold tassels which hang from the bottom of her deep-red, velveted chair. Tracing lighter golds in geometric carpet patterns with my finger, I pull the thick pile backwards against the grain so that it changes over and over to a darker shade of gold. My supersonic hearing tunes into Nan's whispers in the kitchen.

Why's she suh mard George? Dunt wanna play out like normal kids. Why's she jus' wanna be wi' us all' time? It's sunny out theer today.

Grandad snaps back, defensive. *She's a clever un and she's 'appy. Just bluddy leave her to it. She's doing no 'arm. If she wants to read books and knit wi' ya instead of getting hersen in trubble out theer, as alreet wi' that.*

I wonder if it's because we're similar, Grandad George and me. He reads constantly. Newspapers, magazines, encyclopedias. We are crossword champions together. If he doesn't know an answer, I do, and vice versa. I only ever see him go out to play bowls or snooker and he's Captain and champion in both cases, their walls dripping with gold plaques and tournament medals inscribed with his name. Up at the bowling green, they hand me bags of Seabrook prawn cocktail and blackcurrant cordial with ice. *Our team would be nothing without your granda, tha knows.* As well as his job on the buses, Grandad keeps stocks and shares, checking them religiously on Ceefax. He seems to know the horses so well that his 'flutters' often land a new gold ring on Nan's finger or another holiday at the caravan in Blackpool for us all. Everyone says he's so clever. That he really should have gone to University. He says, *that's not fer folk round 'ere.*

One summer when I was seven-ish, we'd stopped to feed apples to two majestic black horses who met us over the barbed wire fence of a farmer's field up near The Dell. They bowed their heads, familiar with Grandad and his trips to see them. He peeled off the sticker and handed me a Golden Delicious, lifting me just slightly so that I could reach to hold out the apple in my outstretched palm. As suddenly as he had taken a bite, I felt my head go fuzzy and warm blood start to pour from my nose. Grandad sat me down on dried, browning grass, reaching for the pale blue criss-crossed cotton hanky he always carried. He folded it quickly and placed it under my nose to catch the drips. I looked down through fuzzy vision to see that some had already dripped onto my dress.

Ee kid, he said, pinching the top of my nose ever so slightly. *Tha's a sensitive one if ever there was one. Here, try this, pinch your nose gently and tip tha head back slightly. That will help it to stop. Plagued wi' bluddy nosebleeds just like me, aren't ya.*

He explained that it would be the heat, that he'd had constant nosebleeds when he'd be sent to Egypt with the RAF. How it had once meant they'd had to land a plane. I felt better then, wrapped up once again in his stories. When it finally stopped bleeding, he held my hand and helped me up, passing the Vimto. *Tha's got to drink plenty after a nosebleed to rehydrate. Come on kid, keep gadding, we'll head back home.*

As we walked back up the last stretch of our walk back from The Dell up cobbled Ladybird Lane, so called for its summer swarms, my hand pulled as Grandad stopped suddenly and I turned to see deep red dripping from his nose now. I squeezed his hand. *Ah, this bluddy heat,* he said, reaching for the reddened hanky to reuse for himself.

At school, in stuffy classrooms, my nose bleeds came on suddenly and from nowhere. I would run down flights of stairs to stinking toilets, hand covering my nose, mouth closed to stop the horrid taste of iron. It was a tricky balance to find, pinching my nose and tipping my head back, just enough to slow the bleeding but not enough so that it would drip down my throat instead, drip, drip, drip and turn my stomach sick.

Nose bleeds, headaches, aching legs, sensitivity to light, smells, noise; constant tummy aches just made me a nuisance. Sometimes I felt so tired that I could drop when others weren't tired at all. On a school trip to Shuttleworth Farm with its droning animal calls and eau de cow, I had led down on a hay bale for a rest after throwing up in the toilet and fallen asleep.

At Uncle Jim's fiftieth do at the social club, I apparently ruined the night after hiding under a tablecloth with my head in my hands, away from painful flashing rainbows and the blare of three-foot speakers.

As time's gone on, I've learned not to make a fuss and just to put up with stomach knots and headaches instead. Getting into trouble makes me feel worse than the loud noises and lights do anyway. I find myself not speaking much either, because when I do, I've become a walking Collins Dictionary. Four and five syllable words spewing like a foreign language onto deaf, unwilling ears.

Candi Martin

Pushing the Envelope

on squat autumn nights — thick with fire & coal
pithy leaves lined the gutters

Nan cut holes
in black bags for my arms when it rained
tied string around my waist
          bodice-tight

we bought ink-stained chips & mushy peas
from Olga's mid-terrace fish & chip shop

after her son had died
she installed a fryer
in her lounge
i remember there was still
carpet on the floor — heavy with grease
& a grey mop & bucket in the corner

the counter glass too-hot-to-touch
          vinegar steam stung my eyes
Nan slapped at my fingers when they
drummed the counter / flashing me a glare

cut to us
stopping by Pat's
on the way home — *she's expecting us*

she'd be holed up in the kitchen
listening to her grey mustard wireless
— old men acting the fool

Nan always carried an envelope
to push across the tacky tabletop
— always the same —
Pat would push it back
my eyes were glued to this feigned refusal

          her husband
a small gent with a thick moustache / sideburns
an open neck shirt / braces / half-moon specs
commandeered their lounge
& read his newspaper in
burning orange lamplight
while his wife
fidgeted — in the margins — with twenty smokes & a lighter
waiting for a friend to call

he choked her with his ashy clouds

when i catch pipe smoke
& vinegar now
i see ghosts

Alan Parry

Send It Through a Body

The door gave way to a middle-aged man. He held something and spoke some kind of patter to my mum off whose hip I stood watching.

Mr Thwaites, he said, shaking my mum's hand. Then he looked at me. Come join us, he said.

I rocked up at church the week after. Mum said goodbye and that she'd be there to collect me later. Don't know if I had a uniform, probably not, think it came piecemeal over the following weeks. Red sweater, pleated shorts. The shoes had to be polished, Mr Thwaites said, and the beret worn like this.

Far as I could tell, we were some kind of organisation with the church to keep kids out of trouble. We played crab-football and marched. We sang and saluted and went to church one week in four.

One evening I sat in my uniform ready for the short walk. Princess Diana was on TV; it might have been her funeral. We listened to Elton John and watched a candle wave. I felt it all. Certainly my grandparents did. They were fixated, while I played with a coin in my mouth. It was a twenty-pence piece for Mr Thwaites.

I had to interrupt the funeral to say I'd swallowed the coin. One moment I was turning it over with my tongue and the next it was sliding down my throat. Cold silver in the gullet—it seemed to last forever. Hours later, it still hadn't found my stomach. This, the fear of being opened up by a surgeon, and the funereal gloom on the telly all made for a frightening cocktail.

Grandma on the phone to hospital. Elton John on mute. Hospital said I wouldn't need to come in, not yet, but gave Grandma some pretty grim instructions. Someone would need to fish through my poo. The coin would come out, they said, over the next day or two.

Probably.

At church (can you believe they still made me go?) Mum told Mr Thwaites that if I happened to go for a shit in the next ninety he'd have to break it up and check it for coin. Fair play to Thwaites; if it was a strange request he didn't show it.

I didn't need a shit. I'm sorry. Thwaites was saved from plunging his pious hands into the toilet. He would not be snapping turds tonight. At least not between the hours of 6:00 and 7:30.

It was my mum who eventually dug it out. A few days later, surprisingly pristine. And shiny. If you want to clean a coin: send it through a body.

What else shall I tell you? That I spent it up the road? That I handed it over for a 20p mix? That sometimes I wonder, these years on, in whose pocket it jingles?

DH Holmes

We have it at home

I peer inside their houses — those sandy-brick towering, wood-tipped houses
those gold-for-a-moment houses I imagine smell like sandalwood and branded detergent
those ones I imagine are owned by happy people
with their pedigree dogs and their affairs and their secrets hidden under floorboards
I peer inside them as they flash past the car window — glass gold for a moment
the rattle-hum-bang 'god knows' noise under the wheels rumbling me to sleep
bringing me to the cusp of some realisation or another —
something about the fine line between me and the sandalwood wives
and their husbands with their fingers in pies — I wish we could linger for longer,
but we pull up on the drive and roll on and on and on
and the rattle-hum-bang of the heating rumbles us a welcome,
the clicking of the thermostat as my dad checks that it's just right —
it's a feel-it-in-your-bones night, where mum runs a bath and wraps me in two towels
dad flicks the heating off when I get into bed, the hum of the TV rolls up the hallway
two rooms away, I breathe in, smelling the soap on my skin as I fall asleep —
and then the realisation — there is everything gold about this place.

Rebecca Riddell

Pleasure Beach, you have the worst of me

Sun-baked path splattered with seagull shit and surrendered chips
between the love boat and the kids zone where I realised I'm too
fat for a summer,
my hulking shadow
swallowing my friends, swallowing the light, swallowing back
sick.

The dizzy turn of a season and a merry-go-round and my twister
gut and you alone on a blue and pink horse.
The spinning shame of being
loved unlovable
I hid in the ghost train; I didn't want you to see any more of
what follows me around.

On the log flume we sat in the back; you gripped my pac-a-mac.
You were feeling it; I was feeling the slip palm sweat laughter wet
on my neck, I hiccup, we go up we go down.

Smell of ice cream
and sunscreen
on your arms
holding me — there are no arms in the world big enough
to hold me —
what if the bar springs up and I fall?
Mr Whippy dripping down your cone.

Later, the last words of love scrawled into the sand
with our bare hands with your dirty hands
the last thing I let you say, my last excuse,
an Instagram sunset on eight years of summer the sea went cold.
Last whoosh of the ride. Last train at the stop.

Emily Mather

Mr Pearl

Mam kept me off school the day they found Dad in a ditch on the Batley Road, his hair and beard stiff with frost, an empty bottle of Haig in his hand. I had to miss gymnastics.

'He did nowt to deserve a decent funeral, but he's getting one,' Mam said, fetching the premium receipt book which Mr Pearl initialled every Friday. 'I won't have folk thinking we don't have two farthings to rub together.'

She always hid the coppers – tuppence for his policy, tuppence for hers – after Dad said he'd no need for Mr Pearl; for all he cared, his mates from The Grapes could chuck him into a lime pit with a keg of Tetley's.

I didn't care either way. As long as that leather strap went with him.

Mr Pearl's tweed overcoat had specks of sea-green in its weave and I imagined his pockets heavy with pearls plucked from the ocean by daring brown-skinned boys. They'd laugh as they held their trophies aloft, flicking the seawater from their dark hair before diving again and again amongst golden coral while angelfish gawped and stingrays threatened.

Mam always had a brew and a natter with Mr Pearl. He'd tell her who was on the sick, whose daughter in the family way, or whose son had been locked up in the Borstal. Six months after the funeral, I came home from practising somersaults to find them a handspan apart on the couch. I hoped he'd woo her with three-row necklaces and let me count the pearls in his pockets.

'Don't be daft,' Mam said, sadly. 'There's already a Mrs Pearl.'

I kept up with my gymnastics so I could join the circus and ride two white horses at once, performing everywhere from Settle to Ceylon. Here, we'd watch the pearl boys dive and I'd choose which one I'd marry, with the ringmaster giving me away and the clowns looking sad when I waved them goodbye to live on the seashore with my husband and brown babies.

It was only the following winter when the influenza claimed Mam at thirty-seven. As the eldest, I took her premium receipt book into the Pearl on Albion Street, but the lady assured me the policy was worthless.

'She'd stopped paying her premium, love.'

I told Mr Oldroyd the undertaker there was no money for the funeral.

His face was as grey as his trousers but he wreathed it into a smile.

'A gentleman came in and paid for everything. Specified two white horses.'

I shivered in the thin sunlight at Beckett Street Cemetery and sprinkled a pinch of earth over the gash in the ground where Mam lay, an arm's length from Dad through the mud. When I looked up, a man was weaving his way through the mourners towards me. Stepping up, he bowed once to me and once to the grave. Through my tears, the sea-green specks in his overcoat sparkled as, together, we showered Mam's coffin with pocketfuls of pearls.

Chris Cottom

Frogspawn

I am ill   prepared   my waterproof does not appear to be waterproof
we are climbing a horseshoe of hills but it is so foggy   I see nothing
but each next bit   grey-purple-early-morning   sleet
small group of humans   so different   held together by one thing
by who we love   I forget then remember and it feels like swallowing
a sacred stone   knowing this intimate thing   about every person
in the middle of jobs and dogs and wainwrights and car-shares and cereal bars

I am ill   equipped and they lend me layers   hat   gloves   socks
let's warm up liz they say   we huddle   behind rocks from sheets of wet
rain changing my being   oozing cold into   toes   eyelids   shoulders
I can make out a round denseness in a stretch of puddle   kneel to marvel
at its intactness   perfect tiny spheres   in this temporary scratch of water
I want desperately to feel it   plunge up to my wrists   it is beyond jelly
it sends something happy shooting to my brain   how it quivers   remains

I am ill   of hate and fear and the internet and how I cannot change myself
mostly do not want to   but there are people out there who wish I wasn't here
I show my group the frogspawn   take photos   later   we find masses of it
glut   I have wanted to use the word   glut   a lone dead frog
floats upside down   pale yellow-orange   toes so long   fine   miraculous
someone asks us to guess how many tadpoles survive to adulthood   we all
guess too high   it is not many at all   they looked it up   we plod on

there are stirrings in the cloud   slivers of green   then there they are
hills   swelling and tumbling   curves of body   resilient in a way
I cannot really comprehend without crying   I am offered nuts and raisins
caramel shortbread   my pupils dilate and they laugh   feed me
the whole world is suddenly a frog   green   rich   here in prehistoric times
jelly egg to   tiny black curl   to muscled spring of movement
I give back the clothes I borrowed   the village is in sight   we will eat together

Elizabeth Gibson

Heaton Chapel

Temperate gardens stretch
behind the houses.

Our own is wild, unattended

except by foxes. All day
next door's husky howls
for his family.

Well-insulated roofs
blanch in January sunlight.
This one eats heat,
and so mould squeezes itself,
black and menacing, between
the glass frames of the paintings
in my bedroom.

The private road is cracked and pot-holed
to measly homeowners.

I am nothing but a tenant.

It has little to do with me.
Pigeons knock about in the gutter regardless.

I'm magnolia paint on the wall,
duveted from the cold,
yawning yellowed through the season.

On the opposite road
a loft extension is nearing completion.
                    Men drill in fair weather while I

                    am wonderfully inanimate.
                    My eyes mere bloodshot

craquelure, thirsting

for the hills far out
on the horizon.

Edward Heathman

Cake of the Day

I
am falling into a spiral of chemistry that has baked
itself
into my genes. It started at birth and finished with us.
My
cells are fighting a slow pleomorphic,
inevitable
end. Do join me

as
I mix up all the remaining pieces of my life
in
the cakes I never bake, in the food I no longer prepare.
I
hide them away till they rot mixed with a
lemon
citrus spike.

They
creep out from behind the cupboards and I stir in
all
the pieces left unanswered, mix them well.
This
new improved cake you will like.
Taste
its foul centre carefully.

I
  make this mandrake pie for myself every day,
and
  take a pill to savour its bitter twist. Its guile is softened
by
  spice and snare and sweat.
                                        I
  allow you the biggest slice.

Karan Heppell

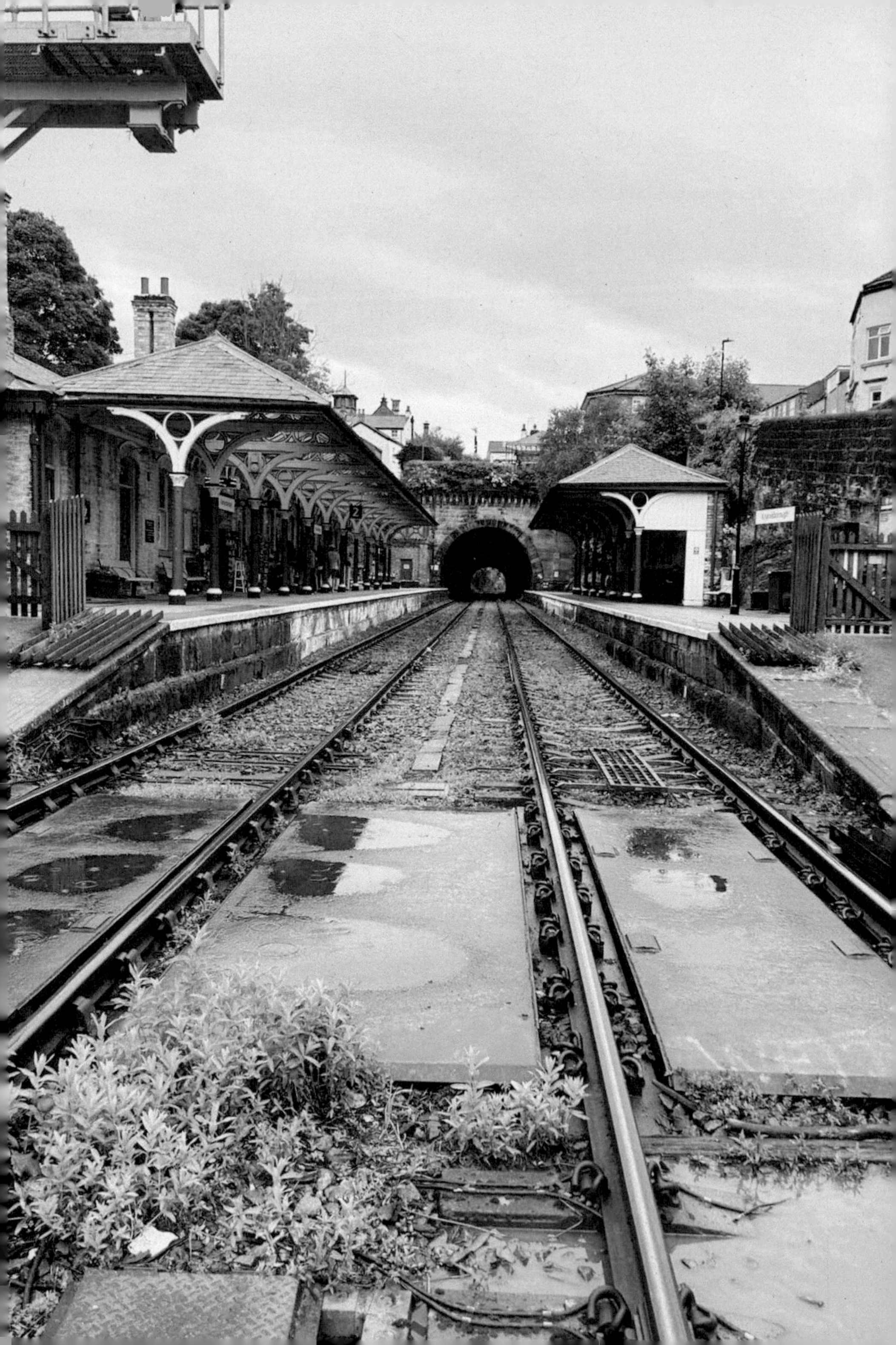
2

The Choice

Seeing her a crumpled version of her former self
Gone the energetic woman who I ran to keep up with
Gone the beautiful sister whom I had known all my life
The body a frail and birdlike image
The mind long gone
She knew me for long after I expected
But then today even that had gone
Hanging on to a life that she cannot make sense of
No longer allowed to eat the treats she enjoyed
Going through the motions of living
I see her and wonder what is in store
Hoping I will be long gone by this
Hoping a choice will be a thing by then:
A thing acceptable
My choice.

Carole Thirlaway

Reflections — Did I Know You?

Did I know you?
What bit of inside you did I know?
You were funny.
To another you were a good listener.
You were many things; you were complex.
Humans are complex.
Life is complex.
Relationships are complex.
Interactions between us are unique
to that connection.
Everyone has a story.
I love hearing stories about the you I did not know.
Surprises spring forth as I discover another facet of you.
I love more of you as more of you is revealed to me by others.
Our stories are part of who we are, so who were you?
I wonder, did we really, really, know one another?
Did you know me?

Margaret Montgomery

The Mirror

"Tell me about despair, yours, and I will tell you mine."
Mary Oliver, Wild Geese (l.6)

Tell me about the boxes in your room,
the horrors that lay inside;
the trinkets matted with lint, his Yorkshire travel guides,
the pictures of the sea.

Tell me how your finger follows over the maps,
mimicking *Aire, Ouse, Wharfe,*
the blue paths those rivers have made for themselves
on their solitary way back to the sea.

Tell me how the breaking of the waves
has always been a comfort
because that's what you feel, too.
The rolling swell, the undertow,
the crash and the reckless drama of it all.

Tell me how you suspend disbelief
each time you put a seashell to your ear,
because you're dying
to hear them like you did the first time
with him, on a scraggly Northern beach.

Tell me what his voice became.
Indistinguishable from the wind,
a howl like radio static
so you can no longer hear him.

Only the crackle of the weather.
The blowing of lint from boxes.

Tell me how you're still finding
your way back to the sea,
tunnelling through sedimentary rock
with salt in your eyes.

Tell me that you know how to get there,
that you've got it memorised
by the soft paper and blue lines
he left you.

Tell me that every time you get too close to it all,
you rush back to land.

Now, put your hand to the rippling mirror
and she'll soothe you like water.

"I know, I know, I know."

Rebecca Wright

That you, Jack?

It took me six weeks to gain my sea legs. Now, I was finding it an unusual sensation to be back on dry land. The docks in Liverpool were dull grey and featureless: in fact, no less featureless than the Arctic Circle in the middle of Winter. I had never known cold like we experienced on those Winter coveys.

I held a cigarette to my lips to fight off the cold of a bitter wind at the quayside. The dock was a hive of activity; we were loading up for the next voyage but it was long, slow work and at present there was no real sense of urgency. Another ship was docked much further down the side of the quay. They were offloading prisoners off war in handcuffs.

Albert, who I was working with, started shouting at one of them. "Well, bugger me. Jack! Jack! Is that you ?"

The prisoner looked over at Albert and smiled a smile of pure joy. "Albert," he responded.

"What the hell are you doing in a Jerry uniform?" The guards didn't seem to mind the two of them chatting.

"Well, it's a funny story, really. I was visiting my uncle in the Black Forest when the next thing you know, war had been declared! And they have conscription over there. Well, I couldn't very well say no or they'd have had me shot, so the next thing you know, I'm in the German Navy. I didn't let on I was English or they'd have hung me as a spy but all those summers in the Black Forest helping on the farm with Uncle Ernst meant I was fluent in German. Anyway, it's been a nightmare and the ship getting torpedoed was really a blessing in disguise. Can you do me a big favour and let the wife know I am still alive? Maybe just keep quiet about the being in the German Navy part, eh."

Rob Wheeldon

The Deckie*

Beyond the horizon at the Humber's mouth,
The clouds hang low while down below
the grey-brown waters heave and race.

Clouds billow and break and show
a clear blue patch, fit to make
and mend a deckie's shirt; that is,

if he ain't lost it in the Corporation Arms
by boozing, pissing his pay up the wall
that he'd fought so hard to bring ashore.

I'll wash his clothes today. No, not tomorrow
when he's back to chasing mackerel
off the Dogger Bank. 'Cos if I wash tomorrow,

then I wash him out of my life, my heart,
my home, washing him into the grey-brown foam
that's boiling, churning, stirred up by the trawler

taking him back to sea from where
he'll not come back but lie there, drifting,
face down under an eastern sky.

GP Hyde

**Deckie: a deckhand on a trawler*

An Unread Letter

Macclesfield, England, April 1942

The paper of the envelope is rigid and substantial. The corners poke and prod her stomach as she moves, reminding her of its presence in her apron pocket.

The post boy had seen Mariam waiting at the end of the road this morning, when the sky was grey and milky. She is there most days now. He doesn't question why she waits for the post 400 yards from her front door. He knows the envelopes as well as anyone. Those particular letters sit heavy in his bag, he feels the weight of responsibility handing them over. He had simply nodded when he placed it into her cold hand and moved on. Later he would hate himself for that. Sometimes he thought it might be kinder to just burn the letters, to not deliver the news. He was as bad as the Germans he would tell himself.

Mariam had turned from the post boy with a heat behind her eyes, hurrying for home. The curtains were still drawn. Charlie was still asleep, that was something. She couldn't protect her son, but she could protect her husband for a little longer.

She busies herself in the kitchen; kettle, tea bag, bread, butter. She astonishes herself, how she can carry on with such banal tasks with the envelope pressed up against her abdomen; where Fred had grown, where she'd carried him and kept him safe for nine months. How long has he been dead, she thinks now. What had she been doing at the exact moment that her beautiful boy had been blown to bits, when the light went out of his eyes forever, how had she not felt it?

She grabs for the table top, panic rising in her chest. An image of dark eyelashes against a soft cheek comes to her as clear as day and bile rises in her throat. Her boy, her baby boy.

She won't read the letter, not yet.

Upstairs, Charlie lies on his back listening to his wife crashing around downstairs. Every morning he wakes before dawn, stays still and silent as Mariam, his beautiful, brave Mariam leaves the house. He presumes she goes to meet the post boy, for news. He pulls himself up to sit on the edge of the bed and realises that his hands are shaking. He is a coward. He should be the one waiting for the letters. But he doesn't. He knows too much. He spent most of 1916 underground writing letters. He knows that *'killed instantly'* could mean they had their jaw blown off and took two days to die. He knows that *'died gallantly like a gentleman'* could mean any number of terrible, horrifying, unimaginably gory deaths as boys who were too young to sign up in the first place cried for their mothers.

He doesn't want to read a letter, not yet.

Holly Baron-Morgan

1952, South Marine Park

My most treasured photograph of you
is two inches tall.
Edges worn and weathered,
dots of light draped across your face,
dark and slim, slick black hair,
your nose oversized and slightly crooked,
like mine, and your teeth strikingly white
even in greyscale,
are all as they have been described to me.
Taken in South Marine Park,
down the road from where we first spoke,
jewel-toned and gentle, you whisper
the story of the deserter,
the lost boy from York,
charming but fickle and stubborn
like me, stepping off the train at
South Shields, salt sea air
biting at his fingers.

J E Neary

It Wasn't a Real Marriage, We Just Accidentally Entangled Our Souls

When you died it felt like the spirits
Had mistakenly made me a ghost
Instead of you.

For weeks I haunted your absence.

In a closed room, people who could talk

For more than a few minutes without crying

Planned your funeral.

Meanwhile I asked a friend to take my photo.
I wanted evidence that my bony arms
Still floated next to my shrouded waist,
My gaunt skull still capable of smiling,
Hollow eyed, dark
shadows where sleep wasn't.

Meanwhile I visited you on a slab,
And you'd never looked more or less real.

Meanwhile
They told me the grave sites were sold in twos.
Your mother and I looked at each other and
She waited
Until I offered to take the future beside you.
And I'd never felt more or less like her son-in-law.

Kai Cohen

Time

If I could give you anything
It would be the gift of time.
For it is not everlasting and
I have been fasting and feasting
Upon it for years.

Your time is over now.
No looking forward
No looking back.

Time is a trap.
It seems fluid and endless.
Like the water from a tap.
And like water, we need it to live,
But I have nothing left to give you.
But if I could, it would be the gift of time.

Susan Berry

Lisa

She died just after Han's first birthday
It wasn't pretty —
All rope and blood and fighting
to breathe. I say that as I imagine it,
I wasn't there.
She died alone.
That's the part that sticks, every time.
You wish clocks could turn
backwards and that the world was not
so harsh. They said she felt too much.
They say I feel too much.
Her favourite song was Solsbury Hill.
We wove it into our wedding playlist
She came over to thank us.
I wish I could hold her hand then.
I wish I could ask her
What the smile on her face meant
Why — her face was happy
but her eyes were sad.
I wish I could take the sad and tie it up in
brown paper and a bow,
bury it deep in the soil to be broken
down. I wish she was still here.

Zoe Gardiner

Electricity

The city centre pub where we sat,
holding hands, had a power surge.
All equipment and lighting
short-circuited, leaving
only salad on the food menu.

The air crackled. The candle on the table
flamed so high it singed a lightning bolt
on the ceiling (which apparently remains
to this day for the naked eye to see.
Though now I'd need my glasses).

Our friends reported seeing sparks
pinballing round our bodies
— from head to toe to fingertips,
the first time we kissed —
like touching an electric eel,
if we'd been cleaning her tank
but no-one mentioned
we needed rubber gloves,
and a rubber mat to stand on.

Dawn Rhodes-Shaw

Memory Echoes

fishnets and miniskirts on a Friday morning train /
getting drunk at 3pm out of nothing but apathy /
wearing shorts in a january downpour /
sunglasses – indoors /
the stench of sweat and weed squeezing through a dive bar /
dancing so freely that the whole club moves away /
dark purple lipstick and split dye hair /
full-sleeve tattoos of spiders eating honeycomb /
hips grinding against mine /
saliva and makeup running down my collarbone /
the sting of the blood vessels bursting on my neck /
leaving the world for a stranger without a second thought /
thinking "this time I can't fuck it up." /
cuddling the bouncer outside of KFC /

being punched by the bouncer outside of KFC /
cleaning up a nosebleed while the cabbie kicks us out /
shagging in her bed with my eyes shut tightly /
seeing everybody I meet as a speck of stardust /
treating them like glass statues /
thinking "I'm really going to fuck this up." /
making love again on a Saturday afternoon /
regretting it the next day /
taking the bus home with my shirt on inside out /
the anger of the roommate I forgot to call /

Daniel Findell

The Outstare

O Mirror, you magnificent sliver--all mouth and no tongue.
Your spine a string, on a rustic nail. For you could witness
mayhem, murder and still remain unbiased. Not filtering
anything. I released you, once--allowed all six feet of you
on top of me, in a gold frame. I got to know myself better,
I caught a glimpse of imperfections through my pupils;
drawing a heart in the condensation with my tongue.
But, you've been captive on the wall for decades, still
keeping my reflection hostage--like a hologram,
eyeing up each move, gesture, with a mortal glint
in your eyes. And then, there's me; the skeleton--
still staring back. Wanting to wipe you clean.

Elliot Chester

Euphoria

Head dangling dangerously close
To the water and my bile
In the porcelain palace
Which holds all my secrets
Eyes closed, I pray
For forgiveness
There's always a price
For that ephemeral high
The irresistible urge
For the white powder
Seemingly sent from heaven
After I've said never again
It overwhelms me, every time
But if I die tonight, tell my love
I'll see him in the next life
And I'll love him more this time
Than the fleeting feeling of euphoria

Vella H

Emotional CV

I had a gap year from dating,
couldn't bear the disappointment.
I was... unemployable, unable
to find a permanent position.

The dim lighting, clinking of glasses,
music raging against my ears.
Bodies crashing against each other
in the pit with angry thuds.

Watchful eyes on the dance floor,
watching the drinkers,
watching the pursuit,
pursuers and the prey.

I did not apply myself,
I did not put myself forward for
promotion or consideration.
I chose numbness over sensation...

Amy B. Garratt

Teignmouth

The wind howls along Teignmouth Pier. The sea is glistening. And its waves are crashing against the Pier's iron frame. Salt is in the air. February is whistling in the distance. A middle-aged couple are sat on a bench a few yards from us. They're chatting away. Happy. Happiness irritates Ciara. Of course it irritates Ciara. Everything irritates Ciara. For Dean and Ellie's sake I'll keep my mouth shut for the next few days. If I haven't walked into the sea by Sunday night.

'How long are they going to be?' asked Ciara. 'I'm freezing.'

'How should I know?'

'Well why don't you go and have a look?'

'No need. Look. They're on their way back.'

'Finally.' She huffed. 'What's up with you?'

'Why would there be something up?'

'Because you have a face on. You always have a face on.'

It's never simple with Ciara; she delights in dampening the mood. She can turn a good evening into a damp squib. Dean says it's a class divide. I'm not sure.

'Fish and chips for you Madame.' said Ellie, handing Ciara a tray.

'Thanks.'

Dean passed me my portion.

'Ta, mate.'

The fish and chips were too hot to eat. But the tray warmed my hands. Ellie and Dean were huddled up together. Linking arms. Ciara's arms were folded. Her head was turned away.

'Anyone fancy a drink?' I said. 'I saw a little wine shop earlier. Round the corner.'

'Wine would be nice!' said Ellie. 'Dean?'

'Yes please.' he replied. Mouth half full of chips.

'Red or White? I could grab a bottle of Merlot? Shiraz?'

'You didn't want to walk round the corner five minutes ago. Now you're a red wine connoisseur!' said Ciara.

'Or I could get a Pinot Noir?' I said.

'Pinot Noir sounds good!' said Ellie.

I needed to get away. The wine shop bell jingled as I went in. The shop was between a Salon and a Co-op. It was quiet inside. Which was indicative of Teignmouth in general.

'Hello.'

'What do you want!?' asked the shopkeeper.

'A bottle of wine.'

'I know that, you prat. It's a bleeding wine shop. What kind of wine?'

'What's your most expensive bottle?'

The shopkeeper's eyes lit up. He disappeared into the back and quickly came back out with a bottle of red.

'2016 Beaulieu Shiraz, Sir. It's £895 for the bottle. Exquisite.'

'Mm, OK. Let me have a think.'

'Absolutely Sir! Look around!'

To the left of the counter was a makeshift aisle, full of cheap bottles. Shiraz. Pinot Noir. Pinot Grigio. Cabernet Sauvignon. I grabbed the cheapest bottle of Pinot Noir I could find. £8 something. I didn't care whether it tasted like shit. I just wanted to drown Ciara's platitudes out. The shopkeeper was peering over at me.

'Thoughts on the Beaulieu Shiraz? It's glorious!' he said.

'I'm sure! I'll just have this one.'

The shopkeeper looked at me distastefully, scanning the bottle.

'That will be £8.75.' he said monotonously.

'Am I OK to pay cash?'

'Obviously.'

'Great! I've just been in the Arcade. Came out with a load of loose change.'

I dropped an obscene amount of copper and silver onto the counter. Mostly 2s and 5s. The occasional 20. That will teach the fucker. I went next door and bought some plastic cups for the wine. Fish, chips and a glass of red wine. Sláinte.

I could see them in the distance. Her blonde hair. His undercut. And Her.

'That was quick.' said Ellie.

'It's only round the corner. I've got some cups too.'

I sat down next to Ciara. She didn't look at me. Hadn't touched her chips either. Suits me. I wish she'd fuck off back to Wycombe permanently. The fish and chips were still warm. They were good, too. The red wine was a nice treat. The seagulls purred. And purred louder along the pier as they tucked into a dropped portion of chips.

'That wine's nice, man.' said Dean.

'Lovely!' said Ellie.

Ciara didn't say a word. At least she wasn't whinging.

'Not sure I'll go back in there for the remainder of this holiday, mind.' I said.

'Why!?' asked Ellie.

'Long story. Doesn't like out-of-towners, I guess.'

The sky was blackening. Our hotel was a ten-minute walk away. I walked in front with Ellie. We moved slowly. Soaking up the Devon air. Dean walked behind with Ciara. He was trying with her. She was just trying.

'I'm not sure how much more I can take of her, Els.'

'Dean did mention it.' said Ellie.

'And what do you think?' I asked.

'Does it matter?'

'Of course it does. I've known you for nine years. I—'

'Well. Are you happy?'

'In general? Yes.'

'No. With Ciara.'

'I can't stand her, man. It's the incessant whining, the outbursts, The sulking. Even her perfume does my fucking head in.'

'What is it—'

'I don't know. Some floral shite.'

'No. What is it going to take for you to end it.'

'She's unstable. I'm trying to get her to break up with me.'

'And that's clearly working.'

'Help me.' I said.

'I will when we're back in Manchester—'

'We're not leaving until Sunday! Ellie!?'

'I'm aware. I booked the trip. You'll just have to lump her whilst we're here. It's either that or a stroll into the sea. And me and Dean would prefer you to stick around,' she said.

It was past midnight. The other two were in their room; Ciara asleep in the bed in that ludicrous pyjama set. I snuck out with the last of the red wine and walked up and down Teignmouth's high street. The streetlights were flickering. The town was silent. I tried to find a pub. I didn't want to go back. But everything was closed. Our hotel had a bench outside its entrance. I sat down and finished the wine. Light drops of sleet began to fall. I stared out at the sea. It was February.

Beck Alexander

Between

In memory of Selina

There is no in-between time,
   now
only do time
what's next time
one speed now
      not fast
no stop
slow
this place of waiting
      watch her move
less

Sleep more
winding down
   trying not to look
      too close

         Pry
not cry
care less
Just Care

Just

Wait

Chris Barras

Breathe Again

Alt 1:
They bite
You snap.
They bark
You lash.
They storm
You rage.
On and on
Until one of you breaks.

Alt 2:
They bite
You...
...pause.
Breathe.
(Silently seethe)
Then
Breathe again.
A breath of kindness,
For yourself,
And them.
What's going on
Under the war of words;
With you?
With them?
Breathe again...

...and ask.

Anne-Marie Draycott

Cheers

January.

Birthday.

A new date, in the calendar.

"Let's go away and celebrate."

We entered the converted barn, approached the bar and removed damp jackets which were swept away and hidden from sight.

"Champagne, glass of red?"

"Shall we get nibbles too?"

The restaurant was quieter than the snug. Ready to read, we opted for the cosy corner. Free hand rested on the other's thigh. A white geranium on the windowsill twisted towards the light.

The house and buildings privately owned. A wealthy aristocratic family home; reimagined, repurposed, reinvented. Five-star hospitality welcomed influencers, country estate aesthetic turned heads, splayed for all to see over glossy pages.

James and Catherine.

Heir and Creative Director.

Husband.

Wife.

The bedroom "Welcome" literature shared a curated snapshot of the world within the estate's walls; an invitation to believe, leave the curtains drawn, please.

They entered the restaurant like firecrackers. The little girl twirled and swirled; her feet tip-tapped on the wooden floor. They chose the plush upholstered bench. Mother and daughter exchanged quickfire snippets. Leather handbag dropped to the spare chair, cashmere sleeves pushed back to elbows, long brunette hair swept over one shoulder. Menu perused whilst fingers caressed her daughter's crown.

Familiar, to an extent. The post-school, pre-weekend wind down. Friday teatime. This little girl donned a crested uniform, probably a straw boater come the summer months. She twittered away to her mum, mummy, mamma, ma-maar. All the same, underneath. The woman confidently ordered items not in print. Unquestioned and further alternatives suggested by the on-hand, attentive, ready to help, maître-d. He regurgitated with urgency and acute attention to detail the order to the eager waitress.

Juice, herbal tea and fresh snacks promptly arrived. The duo sat wedged together, a constant ripple of affection flowed back and forth, back and forth, back and forth. Hair stroked, cheeks kissed, arms embraced, hair stroked, cheeks kissed, arms embraced, hair stroked, cheeks kissed, arms embraced, another child. Daughter number two had tumbled into the room. Longer limbs than her sibling, she wore identical uniform but was accompanied by her dad, daddy, pappa, pa-paar. All the same.

The older girl embraced her mother, the bird-like chit-chatter increased, their reuniting reached an attention grabbing crescendo. Dad stayed stood, silent. Coat on, hands in pockets. The little girls, locust-like, polished off the snacks. No waitress or maître-d reappeared.

A button was pressed, like a movie on rewind. The girls and their father reversed from the set. Their mother, mum, ma-maar left behind. Off-stage something had intervened. This wasn't how it was supposed to be. She pulled her sleeves down and cried. The silent cry, whilst the life you had plays on in the other room.

"I think that's her."

"Who?"

"The woman."

"What woman?"

"That woman, the woman, the wife from the 'Welcome' pack."

Should I sneak behind the curtain and buy her a drink?

She beat me to it.

Dried her eyes and ordered herself a gin and tonic.

Anna Brizzolara

Today I Got Dressed

I should've done it yesterday when summer gasped
her last breath

but I left it too late.

Today I got dressed as the trees began their undress;
as the sky mourned the day.

Broken shells littered the break

and sandpipers curled their beaks into the clay.

Today I got dressed.

Leasowe Bay, Wirral

Lorna Rose Gill

A Spell for Comfort

When casting a spell for comfort,
finding the right light temperature
is just as important as finding the right heat,
so if you don't have any candles
at the very least you want a warm bulb.

Next, gather your implements in the chosen place.
A common setup is: bedchamber, ancient tome, familiar,
although personally I prefer the 'tea and boardgames'
configuration.
Be sure to banish friction.
This may require arcane pyjamas,
so slip on your +1 slippers
and your blanket of protection.

Yawn, but be sure to show your teeth as you do.
We are serious about this comfort thing
and rest requires more strength than you would think,
more than you may think you have,
but you will find it.

I promise you will find it.

Lewis Brown

ghazal for my bondu

What is spilt stays in the street
the roof itself empties onto the street.

When the nails and screws fell
they clattered onto the street.

Your blood and its smell, o bondu!
I found them caked on the street.

The door could not Prevent
police that came from the street.

I'll smile my smile
at the thieves across the street.

Lights are flashing
and shadows shriek from the street.

When your hand is in mine
silence rings from the street.

So what do you think, bondu?
Will I win today's fight in the street?

Mymona Bibi

St. Anthony in the Nail Salon

It's a very Catholic thing,
she says, finding the lost eraser in a jam jar of
pencils. That acrylic smell or shellac smell strips
organic from the afternoon,

And look! She says. Holding it up.

I've asked him
to find things myself. Once a wallet emerged
from the bottom of a child's laundry basket.
Keys, often.

Over a martini later I'll hear a story of keys substituted
by matching keys,
seams and depths of sofa unravelling in answer—

Later, later. I hold my hands to her as still as in prayer. I want her to
make my nails tidy,
to tell me that here,
the saints listen.

Vanessa Napolitano

The Vanishing Victor Grayson

Mr Grayson, Yorkshire politician
went to London
and never came back.
He left his friends
for the river bank
and entered the house of a rival.
Monocled Maundy had motive
to spill socialist blood
but so did depression,
suppression of urges,
repression of war trauma.

And was blood spilled or booze?
The Great War clawed him,
left Grayson a pale shadow
of a great orator,
then a widowed father.
He drank but never forgot.
Labour shrugged off Victor.
Honour was up for sale
and he wouldn't buy it.
Trade seemed safer,
an engineer fixes better.

Maybe he escaped through lovers.
A queer cabal got him out
to Australia, South America
or anywhere safer
in the twenties.
A new man in a new land.
Wouldn't that vanishing act
be a sweet kind of conspiracy?
Except for Colne Valley.
Except for his family.
Except for his daughter.

All we know for sure is that
Mr Grayson, Yorkshire politician
went to London
and never came back.

Owen Townend

Victor Grayson was an Independent Labour Party politician who became MP for Colne Valley from 1907-1910. He disappeared in 1920.

Clowning

I did a clown workshop once
I was bad at it
He told me
That I was calling out to someone that is lost
I should've told him I'm a poet
Not a fucking clown
Grief pays my wages
If my pants are down
It's because I put them there
Exposed myself before your eyes
If my shoes are too big
It's because I am poor
And cannot afford the right size
My nose is bulbous, red from crying
And you'll never find bodies
Under the house
I leave them between pages
For everyone to see

Rosa Wright

Morphine Dream

I often fantasise about
Being back in
Sheffield Hallamshire hospital
When I was ill
Not for the pain
Although it did feel good to feel
Or the toilet mishaps
Or the I can't breathe
Or the not being able or allowed to eat
Or the not being able to wash myself
Or the I can't speak
Or the I can't communicate
Please understand me
Or the I can't colour in the lines
Please hold me
Or the I have too many visitors at a time
Or the vomiting
Or the shitting
Or the ogling
No

I miss that hospital window
And brushing my hair with one hand for hours
And being clapped to reach the toilet
Because it's perhaps the last time
I'd ever not feel the unrelenting need
To be productive

The steady ebb and flow of the machines beeping
A tenacious consolation prize of peace and quiet
Maybe I didn't win but at least I didn't die
When they released me
I didn't realise
I'd never be alone again
And by alone I mean
Not with my emails

Eleanor May Blackburn

An Injury

This was not the general scrape
and graze of narrow copper skeins

that mark the skim of asphalt on skin,
but a right proper scrap. An argument

between limb and path,
tissue ejected from its rightful place.

You watched, terrified as I bathed the wound.
Cataloguing debris and mud

I weeded out rogue flecks,
parted fissures in the numb flesh

and tried in vain to staunch the blood.
It must have been an alarming sight:

half a mother and half a bloody ruin,
raw open gash and leg weeping

as if to mourn the mockery
of its rightful form.

I might have made light
of this corruption of our tender frame, masked

the ease in which we can return
to the waiting, patient earth.

Instead, the simple truth:
I tripped and fell. We do not last.

E.M. Davis

A Journey

I'm on a journey, they say.
It's everywhere.
I was on a journey
Down the M60.
I say down... It's a circle.
But let's not be picky
At a time when the smart motorway
was being built.
It wasn't ideal
We need more lanes!
But what if we break down?
Oh, it's fine;
We can stick a massive red X in the lane and you will be safe.
From a **fucking truck?** I will be safe?
ABSOLUTELY! We have experts on the case
Hormones, pain relief or surgery.
Cut and pasted in every letter and consultant meeting.
Three lanes. No hard shoulder.
But what about my journey
Down the M60?
The extra lane?
The lane for breaking down?
I need a red X
To stop the fucking truck.

Eleanor Dickinson

Match Day

On the train we stand knee-to-knee tight,
like sardines, close-packed, intimate.
The engine's throttle jerks, starts. I feel
smaller than I am.

Someone regrets last night's curry.
We hold our breath, stare at our feet.
A joker spars with our silence,
makes like he's the king pin.

Let's introduce ourselves,
I'm Seb; head honcho, NHS.
In its glass box the emergency
alarm is piqued.

Hi, I'm a poet, I say, but only into the folds
of my scarf, the crease of my imagination.

A young man admits to medical student,
Seb advises oncology.
Oncologists are rare as hens' teeth.

I am a poet, I say, *we are abundant*
as daisies. The train's whistle
drowns me out.

Polo mints: he takes one from a woman
who labels herself physiotherapist.
Group hug; Seb, the student,
the physiotherapist.

Look at us, a golden triangle of the NHS,

he says as he charts the sudden raised
temperature of the crowd.

Joy Winkler

Wandering

I want to be less of less
I was a production of pathways
Meeting between hills that stretch beyond their tops
To clear night skies
I miss the stars
The lack of timely buses, well-funded healthcare
To look through the branches and
Into forever
I don't write nature poems
I have seen a horse
And words to sum one up, the fields they roam, the way they look
Upon each other
Every living creature has its own perception of this world
When I say hello to cats on morning walks
And bid adieu to pigeons
Each one here at different times
Some cats run when you approach
And you can't explain to them exactly who you are
I am glad for better buses
More understanding doctors
But I would like to see some stars

Fee Marshall

Parting Gift

I saw you once,

hurried nightward, dragging the chill in the tail of your overcoat. Walt Whitman on Athenaeum street, a moth to the flame of day. I heard you were out looking.

I thought this city looks well on him, its pavements draped over him like threads of some ancestral robe, its backwaters pooling in his greying eyes. I heard the clop of your Oxfords on the boiler room floor, the steps of a proud working father, the sound of your hands drinking shyly from the tap. I found the wintry ends of your beard in the shopping centre sink. I'd have painted you a bridge to cross, but I think, deep down, you would have slept where it rises in the middle, where you'd be eye to eye with morning's chirp. You'd have taken a nightcap from the seething clouds, hung your lungs across the balustrade to dry, filled your ears with hawthorn and bid goodnight inwardly. And in due time, as you daily did, you'd have let the morning dress you in your Sunday best, and walked back the way you came, a suitcase hanging from each finger. You'd go on your way to meet someone who looks like you at twenty, someone you had seen about, staring. Off to die unseen in your bed.

I hoped somebody told you then, you always looked impeccable in the malady they gave to you; your parting gift the day you blew a kiss to centres, to chase the shapelessness of love -

the kind that rains ruinous everywhere

i.m. The Bag Man of Sunderland

Grace Copeland

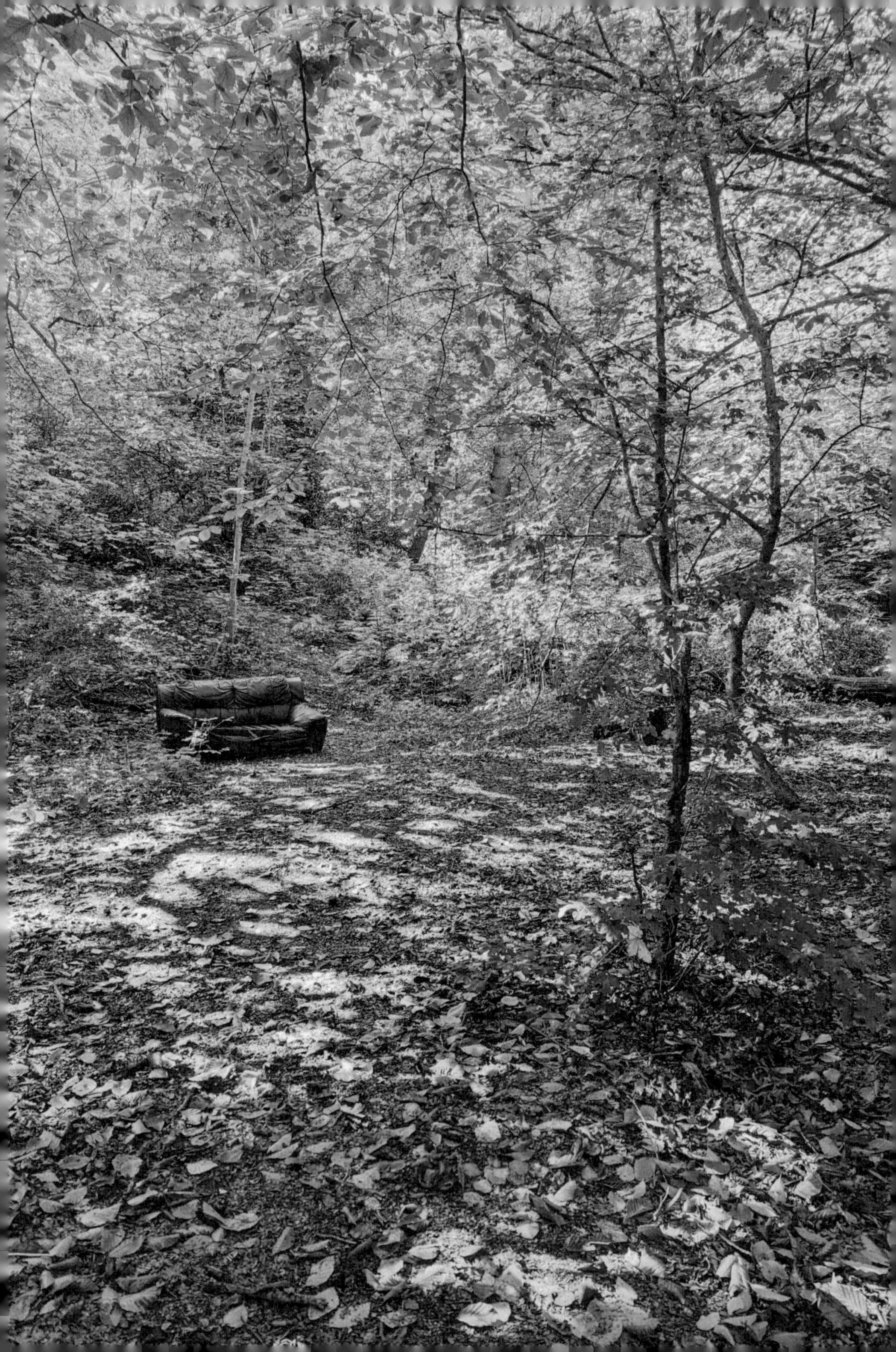

Bella and Bertie

With heads held high and posture bold
They guard and they survey
Legend has it the city would vanish
If they were to fly away

Standing tall and proud at eighteen feet
Their copper hue now green
If their elegant beaks could talk
What would they say they'd seen?

Bella's gaze meets coast, sea and port,
Guides ships and sailors home
Outstretched wings welcome to safety
You'll be treated like one of her own

Bertie overlooks the city, the land,
The buildings, and the houses
Admired for over a hundred years
By tourists and by Scousers

This iconic duo atop their grace
A feather in the cap
Of a City that stands up for itself,
It soars and does not flap

Many more in this image exist
But this pair are best known
So when you look at them, remind yourself
You'll never walk alone!

Jen Corcoran

Teacakes at the Border

Growing up in Carlisle, right on the Northern border of England, I knew our kind of Northern wasn't the same as everyone else's but I didn't think about it much, except to feel excluded not just from mainstream England but from all generic Northernness. To put your finger on it you have to go into specifics. Such as Coronation Street: Coronation Street is meant to be northern but you had to drive south for two and a half hours to get to Manchester from my house. Such as teacakes.

Standard English teacakes are largeish, flattish bread buns shot through with currants, which you mainly get in cafés. You bite in and three things happen, all at once. The toasted edge of your teacake crunches; meanwhile the bread underneath offers a chewiness that pops with sweet-warm currants; and all the time there is melting butter, than which nothing is more delightful. These days they are an indulgence somehow more virtuous than a cupcake, closer to real food.

But for us at the border, teacakes are not that. West Cumberland teacakes are the teacakes we had with high tea at Gran's, when there was ham (sometimes tinned, sometimes from the butcher's, pink and then a strip of white fat and one of yellow breadcrumb coating), beetroot from a jar, tomatoes, cucumbers, hard boiled eggs, round lettuce (in those days the only lettuce to be had in Cumberland) and plenty of salad cream – a table heaving with good things (and with Bird's trifle to follow). The bread at this feast was teacakes. These are similar in size and shape to the classic English teacake, but there the similarity ends. No currants, no toasting, and you slice them from top to bottom, giving fingers of varying lengths, and then you put plenty of butter on them. They need it because the bread's a bit dry (unlike its northeastern counterpart, the stottie cake). When I was a child this was what a teacake was.

Had I grown up ten miles further north, however, in Scotland, a teacake would have come wrapped in foil. It would be a thin base of shortbread smeared with an even thinner layer of red jam, topped with a dome of soft meringue and the whole dipped in that kind of cooking chocolate that isn't quite the shade of brown that chocolate should be. They are the sort of thing expats will have shipped to Spain along with their baked beans and marmite.

The word *teacake* in Cumberland happily represents all three kinds of food. We don't take up arms against the ersatz Scottish invader, we don't mock, we just have them all – although there is an undercurrent (undercurrant?) of disrespect for the standard English teacake because it is soft and sweet enough for southerners to be able to cope with, much like their weather. The Tunnock's tea cake, however, is at once Scottish and ours. Because we are borderers. And it's almost as if we don't notice that we use the same word for two completely different things. On the border we live in our own world that we know isn't mainstream England. We know we're different, we're made to feel different every time we engage with the rest of the world; but we know as well that if anyone's different, it's them. It's just that they don't realise it.

Hilary Elder

Take Me Home (to Stockport, Yeah)

Take me home.
Take me home to where the Heron flies,
So I can see familiar faces,
In the ripples of the River Mersey.

Take me home.
I want to feel the life,
Of these Northern Deities,
Flow through city streets,
Like roots of a family tree.

Take me home.
So I can hold close, those dearest,
That they might imbibe my love,
To share with thy neighbour,
Close their eyes,
See a city in cultural bloom.

Take me home.
Home to where I leave my heart to break,
Where I raise myself in my family's name,
Phoenix ashes destined for more,
Holding close votives,
Of an ever changing,
Ever evolving hive of workers.

Take me home.
To be close to you,
Feel the hum of your fluttering chest,
As we waste summer days,
Pollen drenched afternoons,
Suckling nectar from those generous plants,
And watch the sun dip,
Dip, dip behind the Underbank.

I am Home.
Inscribed on the walls,
Where I scrawled graffiti as youth.
Held in the soil I sowed my future in.

I am Home. Isn't that beautiful.

James Jackson

Travel by Bee

I saw a woman doing her makeup on the tram this afternoon
The way she held the small compact mirror in front of her like a canvas
Angled the brush ready to strike her lips
Like watching an artist paint a masterpiece

On a busy morning commute a man places a boiled sweet in his mouth
His tongue slaps around it
Like he's licking a stamp to a faraway country
Unaware the noise travels all the way to the end of the tram and back again
A bee flies back and forth into the glass
Aching for the sugar

After work I saw a group of girls giggling as they did a TikTok
Using the yellow handrails to prop themselves up
The innocent smiles that passed between them
As if they were the only people on the tram

I saw a woman fast asleep on the tram this morning
The nights she must have seen
Her coat wrapped tight
Pulled right up to her chin
Like a blanket swaddling an infant
Peaceful for the time it takes to travel from one stop to the next

Life happens on these thin tracks
Honey trails run far and wide
Converging to the hive that is our city

Some memories are more delayed than others
Yet we wait with patience
Always ready for our next destination

Grace Ward

Stranded in Stalybridge

The conductor announces wearily
That the train is about to terminate
Our fate has been determined by a flood on the tracks
Some place up ahead
So we decamp down onto platform two
Some passengers amble slowly, pondering what to do
I scoot through the underpass, amass my options
My soonest is the ten thirty
If I'm lucky I'll be away in twenty-seven minutes
Meanwhile, I'm stranded in Stalybridge
Closer to Manchester than I am to home
And that's about all I know
But, it's a sunny autumn day
A blue sky blue day
The automated station announcer claims my train is on its way
We'll see; I can wait.

I take a seat under a huge clock
Tick-tocking
Suspended in the ornate station
Amongst the wrought iron framework
It's then, in the silence
Between announcements
And overheard telephone conversations
That I notice a tree shedding its Autumn yellow
It's not the sight though
It's the sound as they float down
Into the sea of leaves that weave among the boney roots
It's like a bonfire crackling
You can hear the brittleness as they gently die.

Within this soundtrack, I wonder to myself
Is this where Paul Simon wrote 'Homeward Bound'?
Maybe his train was delayed that day
And the words floated though his head
Sat on this very same gnarled bench
Tapping his Cuban heeled boot
To the tick-tocking clock
Another day, another town, inspiration found
Wait, come to think of it
I think that was Widnes train station
Scratch that thought.

Gary Bunting

Crowing Cocks

They bumped and jeered and jostled her
Stale ale breath in her face as she buried her head into oblivion
Willing the tram to just go faster, to just get her there
To spring her to safety.

And her eyes pleaded with the other passengers
Silently bargaining for the slightest accidental interruption
And her eyes met mine, but I denied her saying
"Woman, I do not know you"

A little later I sat coiled in company, shoving out dry laughter and inhaling sticky anxiety
As the rape jokes flowed, and decorum withered
And the whole night suggested things that nestled right beneath my flesh
But manifested in my sewn-up throat as laughter.

A stroke of the arm, saying "boys will be boys"
And he told me that if I was one of those "women's lib types,"
Then he could end it.
Have a quiet word with the guys.
And they'll probably tone it down if I am offended.

But I gulped down painful bile, and placed
A reassuring hand on his,
Saying, "Man, I am not"

And after about an hour, still another insisted, saying
"You'd be prettier if you smiled more,
You've had a face on all night."
So I threw back my head and obliged
The teeth that should've been grinding and gnashing
Simply sparkled pleasingly under disco lights.

And in the final denial of myself I said,
"Man, I do not know what you are talking about."

And immediately, while he was still speaking over me,
The rooster crowed
And I remembered how the purpose had called out to me
On this day and every other;
"Before the rooster crows today, you will deny me three times,"
And I went home and wept bitterly.

Kate Hook

39. What She Said to Silvas Capitalis*

Inspired by the classical Tamil love poetry, akam poetry

In the forest stands a head
its mouth and eyes an opening.

Hollow me out like this
piece me together with no skin, no bones.

Make me entirely out of larch,
let my nerves be pine.

Ilisha Thiru Purcell

**a sculpture in Kielder Forest by the American artists SIMPARCH. It is made of approximately 3000 pieces of European larch.*

The Sharrow Arrow

I locked the front door, shoved the key under a plant pot and went through the usual runner's routine, double tying my shoelaces, waiting for the bleep on my Garmin to signal it knew where I was, made a half-hearted couple of stretches and set off towards London Road, criss-crossing the terraced streets, plodding steadily, waiting for my breathing to settle.

Just as I turned onto the main road, a lass came out of a side street and paused at the traffic lights alongside me. Tiny, slim as a reed, with a long blonde ponytail, black shorts, snazzy orange trainers and a Pride singlet. She turned and flashed me a smile and a nod before the lights changed and she strode ahead, a runner's tribal expression of recognition and acknowledgement. I ran behind, admiring her easy stride and tattoos, an intricate fretwork of chrysanthemums and monsters snaking up one leg and down one arm.

She loped along easily in a graceful metronomic stride. I knew I wouldn't be able to keep up with her but it would challenge me to try; I was always a lazy runner when I trained on my own.

The odd car slowed down and a few men outside the chicken shop turned to gawp. When I first started running in the 80's, I ran at night for years under the orange sodium glare of streetlights, too embarrassed to run in daylight and be catcalled and shouted at by men. It seemed daft now, to prefer the risk of being raped and murdered at night than be humiliated in daylight.

I'm middle-aged now, and don't give a shit who says what to me, or who's looking at me. I'm running for myself and have taken up my place in the world: in the male space. I run in a shapeless grey vest and leggings, hair scraped back, enjoying the trickle of sweat creeping down my back.

It's a quietish August Bank holiday Monday, but there's a fair few folk about. I dodge a woman in an emerald-green shalwar kameez, wheeling a screaming baby in a pushchair, and two teenage girls in Blades football shirts, vaping like dragons with spiders for eyelashes. I plod past the cafes, the restaurants and the bars, the phone shops and bookies. When I first started running round here, all the old pubs were still open, and there were still a few little factories working. The litter is still the same though: bottles and cans, paper, plastic and dog shit drift at the side of the road, gathering in satellites around the drain grids.

And then a car slowed down ahead, brake lights flashing on suddenly. A white BMW with a lad leaning out the passenger window at the front, shouting something at the running girl, pointing at her rainbow vest. He had badly dyed, fried-looking hair and was wearing a silver puffer jacket, even though the day was turning muggy and hot. She turned briefly and by this time I was close enough to see her face in profile; she looked calm, composed. She had slackened her pace long enough for me to see there was a lad in the back as well. He was leaning out of the window so far, the whole of his upper body was completely out of the car, and he was holding a can of lager. A bus sounded its horn and overtook the kerb crawling car, engine whining as it accelerated.

I'd planned to turn off here and run up Bramall Lane, but I suddenly felt like I should stay here and follow this girl: protect her. She could easily have done what I would have done when I was younger, dodge up a side alley or into a shop just to get away, but she carried on running calmly, smoothly, hardly breaking pace, the glossy gold ponytail flicking from side to side in the weak smoggy sunshine.

The car sped up and I felt a wave of relief. They had gotten bored and were going to piss off, but then it slowed again and waited for the lass to catch up with them. I was close to them now, puffing hard. The lad in the passenger seat at the front wasn't that young, I could see now. He was probably forty, and he was irritated by not getting a reaction. But she must have said something because then his face screwed up into a red ball of mottled flesh, like corned beef, spit forming at the corners of his mouth. I wished I had brought my phone with me. He threw the can at her feet and it exploded upwards, the foam spuming up over her shins, then spinning into the gutter.

"Fuck off, cunt," he said to her, casually, almost as an afterthought.

The car moved forward again, glacially. Up ahead, I could see a set of temporary traffic lights on red, and smell wet, hot tar. A cloud of black smoke was huffing out of a wagon that was blacktopping the road. The car stopped at the back of the line of stationary traffic. The lass — instead of taking the opportunity to run past — stopped level with the BMW. I silently begged her to move on, get out of the way of these dickheads. They were all leaning out of the car now, gibing her, giving her grief, furious at her femaleness, her confidence.

I pulled up right beside her, waiting, pleating my sweaty hands, hovering, not quite sure what to do next. Then she unzipped the running bumbag at her waist and pulled something out: a slim, black plastic folder like a bus pass holder. She opened it and held it out to them, an offering in her small, freckled hand, and I realised what it was with a stab of joy. A South Yorkshire Police warrant card.

"Nah then, lads" she said, smiling.

Brigid Griffin

The Pit

Blackened days, soot-filled rest
Sleep was weak and torn
Child of days gone by
Accepted fate when born

Shaft hung like a shadowed ghoul
Drawing its victim down
To the depth hell would turn away
In poisonous air, drown

Chair not rest in learned place
Paper will see no ink
A child would drag its feet each morn
No time for their minds to think

Who would send this mite to shift?
When light still does not blink the eye
Their long day with weak reward
No time for coins to buy

Line filled and space tight
Hours without notice, slide
Weakened frame, no flesh to glue
No place for peace to hide

Thoughts sought in sky of grey
When flowers replace the grit
Now all that remains in place
Are memories of the pit

Andrew Mears

The Trade

'I'll tell yer sommat else an' all,' he said, twisting the white plastic bag in his hands like a magician distracting his audience, 'I'm not looking for'ard to two weeks' time when't green air regs come in.'

He placed my chicken breast and eggs delicately on the glass counter top, betraying the strength of his thick fingers achieved through thirty-plus years of working with meat, fish and all manner of other produce.

'How do you mean?'

'Well, it'll be a nightmare trying to get any business in. Already tough enough as it is, what wi' John Lewis shuttin',' he said, pointing behind me in the direction of the defunct building despite being inside his own shop. 'Think how many people aren't comin' to the city now. All't footfall has gone. And where's it gone to?'

'I don't...'

'Meadowhall, that's where. You can't do right for doin' wrong.'

I'd gone for a walk down The Moor. I wasn't on the rota that day, a common conundrum for many of the modern working class (or 'working people' as they're very cleanly regarded by the Labour Party nowadays, as if the phrase 'working class' will evoke images of violent revolutions and red flags) — simultaneously there are never enough staff, but also not enough hours to give. Schrödinger's contract, if you like. A new cafe had opened up next to a Costa, and Debenham's sat comatose overlooking the high street.

'Take the £30 order I get every Thursday. 'E's been coming years. Y'see outside there? Used to be a two-way street. Now you've got to use the ring road. Well, 'e's got to come outside the city, past Derek Dooley Way, back out again then all round't big roundabout past the train station. Why would you bother? There's another customer base gone, an' I don't blame him, mi'self.'

'How you goin' to go on, then?'

The Moor Market is older than time itself. Or it certainly feels that way. I am still amazed at how any of those stalls are still in business, cheap as they are. I'd like to think there's some sort of nostalgic magic in the foundations that keep Sheffield's most well-known market going, life support or no. Maybe I dream too much.

'— don't get me wrong, pal, I'm all fo' this green revolution and all that cobblers, but how is it helpin' me when less people will drive into't city and there's no car parks? It's Meadowhall again — y'mean to tell me, all them thousands o' cars there are helpin' wi' them clean air targets they're allus goin' on about? Net zero, all that. There's no point us bein' open all year, way it's going. You know, like they do at the seaside when't shutters are down half the year? That'll be us soon enough, just you watch.'

'Can't council do something for you?' I ask. The second the question is given life, I hear its naivety, and wish I'd kept quiet.

'It's them that's done it, lad. They wain't think properly, or ask us that's been here thirty-three years first. No, they'll just go for what gets the headlines.'

He put his hands out as if about to catch a ball. 'Yer see, what it is, they want all green spaces, but unless you do sommat about transport, routes and fares — y'know, make it easier for folk to get into the city to actually spend their wages — you might as well stay at home and do it online so some poor bugger can slug it round all day in a Tesco van.'

'Large steak pie and these eggs, duck.'

'£5.25, my love,' he responds to the woman without breaking stride.

‘Thank you —’

‘It’s like my lad, he’s just started goin’ out properly for’t first time and even he’s bored o’ the city. There’s nowt here. Y’want to make a day out of it, but why bother? Might as well go t’Leeds instead. They could at least see how they do it, these councillors scratching their heads. It’s rotten and I’ll be honest wi’ yer pal, it’s bringing back bad memories. Anyroad, that’s £12.80 when you’re ready.’

Charlie Parker

Lasagne and Laces

Red brick bunks and blue windows
house those little ghost children
Four am ground beef for my lasagne.

Floating through these moon-trapped paths.
There is little need to return to my space
there is little need not to buy laces too

He should be somewhere round here; I left him somewhere round
here.

Checked the quay, only to find a cat purring its rat,
fish silver-lined and floating to the sky
There is little sense in returning to cook
there is little sense in flying
Under the wicker, a slight tugboat is parked by the road
used to float down the quays:
stolid, still and caerulean.
Two figures fell there, sunk,
fabric festoons the ladders
There is little point in returning;
there is little point in finding him
Bricked-up red-brick children
still stand and wave when I pass again
There is little point in letting them out
Boarded up windows
They're closed for a reason
Little maelstroms that procure
tiny tempests in their whirlwind house
They don't cook lasagne at four.

Moya Ozyer-Key

Longing

When you long for the sea,
you do what you can.

You seek out lakes, ponds, streams,
revel in the pounding sound of rain on concrete
allow your head to be filled and cleared,
by the screams of lost seabirds on the howling wind.
The very molecules of your skin
reach out for signs of moisture, drenched,
in a need to be enveloped in wildness.
You watch the ripples form on still water,
a reminder
that the wind is always present, always
bigger than you, more purposeful.
Your head swims with joy and disappointment
As your body bobs lightly in placid pools
Buoyant, supportive, but not wild.

When you long for the sea
you close your eyes
take a deep breath
convince yourself you can smell salt and feel peace.
When you long for the sea
you remind yourself that you are mostly water,
isn't it natural that your cells cry out to return?

When you long for the sea
you try to remember:
the sea also longs for you.

Natalie Cooper

The Seagulls Came

A long way from sea and yet they came, the seagulls,
In their droves, circling the near empty car park.

Pure white from a distance, heaven sent.
I watched this choreographed display from a café window,

Filling the early morning sky with music, these angel wings,
Gathering the belongings of a life well-lived.

I sat still as time slowed to the pace
Of an assembling raindrop.

Watched until these angels left one by one,
My coffee, now drained of warmth,

The café, now empty of noise,
Everything paling into something,

Significant to me, so much so I could feel
My body floating, carried by the wings

Of a masked dove,
An epiphany to my own existence.

A feeling that was truly mine.

Sarah Cain

January Light

January 2021 – the Dee estuary at Thurstaston, low tide

I don't know why
the world is so beautiful.
I only know that yesterday
with the sun setting over the estuary,
the beach lined by light and shadow
and the long slow waves
of sandpipers taking flight,
I started asking questions again
about the wealth we have
all around us - gold in every
stone and grain of sand -

Who says that the world can't
hold our wildest dreams?
Or that one dream achieved
on the other side of the world
means one less chance for you?

And walking out one afternoon
to find the sun as orange
and wholly glowing as a yolk,
the land broken open and
shining out to its furthest limits;
given the recklessness
of beauty in this world,
on any given day -
what wouldn't you dare ask for?

I don't know why the world is so beautiful,
but isn't it as if,
by loving it
we would become
beautiful ourselves?

Charlotte Walker

Struan

we put our sea-cold feet on sun-warmed rock
calm our busy minds on the gentle shore
decide if we want to live by the sun or the clock

we take turns at talking, you on the tick, me on the tock
link fingers, lost to the sea's quiet roar
we put our sea-cold feet on sun-warmed rock

we watch the boats come in to dock
and I tell you, this is it. I'm sure.
decide if we want to live by the sun or the clock

we scour the beach for shells, find two pennies and a rusty lock
three worn down shards of sea glass, another, then one more
we put our sea-cold feet on sun-warmed rock

me in my jeans, you your favourite summer frock
dressed the same as ten years ago, almost kids, before
decide if we want to live by the sun or the clock

we leave belongings across the sand — a towel, your hat, my sock
breadcrumbs of our day, bound for the sea floor
we put our sea-cold feet on sun-warmed rock

decide if we want to live by the sun or the clock

Amy Frances

How many pigeons in the cree?

How many pigeons in the cree?
Wor family loves them more than me!

Just like those pigeons, I wanted to soar,
This caged little bird,
Needed to see more.

How many pigeons in the cree?
Those pigeons needed to fly, just like me.

Just like those pigeons, I wanted out,
But home was always cooing
When adventures offered nowt.

How many pigeons in the cree?
A life far from home isn't really me.

Just like those pigeons, I've travelled far and wide,
But the North is my compass,
I'm now back by its tide.

How many pigeons in the cree?
I've made it back hyem. It's where I'm meant to be.

Lyndsey Dickinson

Remains

They lie untouched
from years gone by,
different ages,
lots of decay,
twisted interlocking joints
broken pieces spread
amongst the graves.

These bones full
of history from
an age past,
wonders and horrors
in lives,
young and old,
memories hidden
until now.

The battlefield
now so quiet.
Experts gently
remove and examine
what's left,
records made,
time to lay
these people
at last to rest.

Barbara Callaghan

A Roadmap for Home

I can hear what you're thinking,
it keeps me up all night.
The graffiti in the subway
is a roadmap for home.
Telephone lines string
our hearts together.
Find a space
to make our monuments;
fill the sky up from the ground.

Andrew James Murray

Swallowed by the Norf

With *Big Smoke in rear view*, I transverse
on glottal lilts that cease to rust.
I fly on four wheels up the M6 Toll
and imagine

I'm a bird in murmuration. But, I'm
not. I'm in this wheel box listening
to The Jam—and man—it speaks
to me

for now. As Brum hums by in traffic
spew, I soar without feathers towards
cooler climbs. The South is now
a fading vision—

I'm in migration. The Potbanks
clank, the Hacienda calls in haunting
waves, and my shoulders swagger
to a new

beat. *Jam* makes way for *Roses*.
Soot-stained *Waterfalls* hit
my ear holes with force,

I'm swallowed, swallowed up,
swallowed up

by the

Norf.

Dan Hughes

Fly Paper

I watch you, stuck, on the revolting three-inch gluey string that dangles down from the stained ceiling. I sit, silently mesmerised by you, with a creeping unease that feels like a massive presence in the room, despite you being the size of a toddler's thumbnail. My hand moves to my mouth as I ponder on what to do, twisting my lip between my thumb and forefinger. That feeling so many of us have had; uncertainty, indecision, inner conflict.

My eyes absorb the image as a gurgle of responsibility expands in my stomach, getting bigger like the soapy, iridescent liquid globes blown from a bubble wand as kids shriek with joy on a hot summer day. I see you, stuck on the murder weapon, amongst tens of already dead flies, captured by a silent, sticky assassin. Your legs move quickly, in a desperate, futile attempt to escape. Surrounded by the carcasses of your species, your instinct kicks in. Fight for survival.

I sigh. Do you know your fate? Like a prisoner on death row.

I remain looking, waiting for the homeowner to return. Shuffling in my seat, I inhale and look out the window. Like iron filings to a magnet, I'm drawn back to you almost immediately. Staring, watching you. The uncomfortable feeling rising, I grit my teeth and wish it would hurry up and be over. I remain seated whilst wondering if I could help. Even if I wanted to, could I make a difference? Surely there will just be another fly that lands, another trapped by the sticky silencing life-smotherer.

The moral dilemma.

I inhale the guilt along with the stagnant air that smells of rotten food and sleep. Uneasily, I sit, trying not to look again. Hard for someone who always wants to help in some way. For someone who's been there, perhaps.

Because we could all be that fly. Stuck, not sure if we will make it. Uncertain if we will get out, escape, survive. Surrounded by death, doom, and darkness. Trapped, with hope fading like childhood memories. Fighting, frightened, fatigued. If not us, it has been others. The world is full of people stuck. People needing help from strangers, society, and the entire planet.

Stuck.

What do we do when others need us? Think about it. Talk about it. Do something? Do nothing? What use is our contribution—we're only one person? How many times have you heard that? Said it?

I remain seated, selfishly wishing time away. I don't turn my eyes back to the strip of death above my head again. I know the fate of the fly and I choose to ignore it. I don't glance at the vile executioner to see if the tiny legs of the insect have surrendered and become forever still. The battle for survival ceasing. No fight, no hope.

I don't look again, but the thought remains with me—we can all be that fly.

Helen Aitchison

Coffee

One day someone will feel like a hot mug of coffee
when you kept picking up
the cold, half-drunk mugs
hoping to find warmth inside

You thought — something's better than nothing!
as you sipped the lukewarm liquid at best stone cold at worst
It gave you a caffeine fix nonetheless
but left you feeling unsatisfied

One day someone will hand over a steaming cup
with just the right amount of milk
every sip will be hot enough
to warm you to the core

And you will sit with your hands around its radiating heat
feeling protected against
the cold, cold world.

Joanna Kay

Powerful

You want me to feel powerful,
You want me to be strong, but
I find words too hard to express, words
Too hard to speak, my mind runs
One thousand miles an hour with lists
And jobs I need to do, as a woman,
I fight for my place, my seat
At the table of men, I shout
And disrupt in order to be heard,
My opinions, deemed weak,
Invalid, to men, I find,
You want me to be strong,
You want me to feel powerful, well,
As a woman I am powerful, I fight,
My limits expand, the words,
They flow more freely, my mind slows,
The lists and jobs diminish, as a woman,
I fight for my place, I fight for my seat,
At the table of men, I let them know,
I make them aware, as women,
We are powerful.

Lexus Luke-Walsh

Fi

Fi, when you sleep, I knit your breath into a love letter. Fi, I do not know how you can smile so loudly. Remember when boys tugged our bra strings like flat guitars, poked us to compare sizes. Fi, you would spit them out like toffee. Tug them back.

I look for you in every barstool. Laughing like it's wrong Laughing like it's the only thing that's right Fi, it's only right because you are in it.

Fi, I do not know how you can smile so loudly while you're falling. Fi, we are all falling. We are all losing every day to a body that doesn't want us, but I sign every dotted line with the twist in your spine, proudly.

Remember when we had breakfast in that rickety caf. Bulging like it was about to throw us into the canal. It was the staff who didn't wait for your talker to load. Next table on coughing up impressions of you. First time I saw them crack you, Fi. Tears falling like eggs on the table. And I could've turned that kitchen inside out, rocked it on its toes, landed us so far underwater you'd find your smile tangled in its beads.

Instead, I just held you like an awkward haircut.

You are in every song, sitting on the melody like a karaoke hangover. My body packing the beat into its folds. Fi, I could go my whole life only ever listening to you.

Fi, when you sleep, I knit the air around us into an apology. Fi, remember when they laugh at you, you are everything they are not. Laugh louder.

Fi, you always laugh louder.

Ellie Spirrett

Eulogy

When it finally passed there was no announcement
on the six o'clock news. The flags continued to flap
at the end of their poles. A notice went up
outside a gallery: today Working Class Art died.
It had been ailing for years; had been fed
an unhealthy diet due to rising food prices and
had been breathing dirty air. During the pandemic,
while some art grew fat and robust, while ballet dancers
practiced in kitchens and the nation baked bread, working
class art was fighting to survive in a small flat,
working two jobs and caring for its elderly mum.

But it had survived, until now.

A crowd began to gather outside the gallery at four.
They didn't bring flowers or balloons or cards.
They didn't light candles or hold hands. Instead
they brought poems, scribbled on receipts and the backs
of letters — poems which showed the light which
squeezed through the cracks of a difficult life.
Poems which said yes, but this is what we can do.
They brought paintings of streets and shops and flats
and people, of bent backs and hidden scars. They
brought music, played on second-hand instruments
and stories about ordinary lives. They brought all of
these things, the intention to remember and celebrate.
The intention to show that even though, on that day,
working class art had finally succumbed to a protracted
illness, nobody could claim that it had never existed at all.

Karen Kendrick

The Ballad of a Town Called Reaper's Flow

A town that wore a peaceful face
Was not as it appeared.
For, on some nights there stalked a beast,
And their cattle disappeared.

'Don't speak of it', they told themselves,
'Insurance — it will be.
A gift to keep The Beast subdued.'
Blind eyes refuse to see!

The Beast though was not satisfied,
He craved a greater prize.
A babe one night he stole away
And no-one heard her cries.

Harsh light of day revealed the crime
That was too high a price.
The Town was not prepared to give
A child for sacrifice.

Men fury-filled and carrying
Homorphus amulets,
Commenced the hunt with hate in heart,
And guns, with silver bullets.

The Townsfolk found their enemy.
The kill was unrestrained.
Their freedom though was bittersweet:
Their destiny unchanged.

The Beast had left a legacy.
A Lykos child to nurse.
The cycle would begin again.
A fatalistic curse.

This town that wears a peaceful face
Hides well what can't be shown.
Their secret always must be kept.
For she is of their own.

Julia Ellis

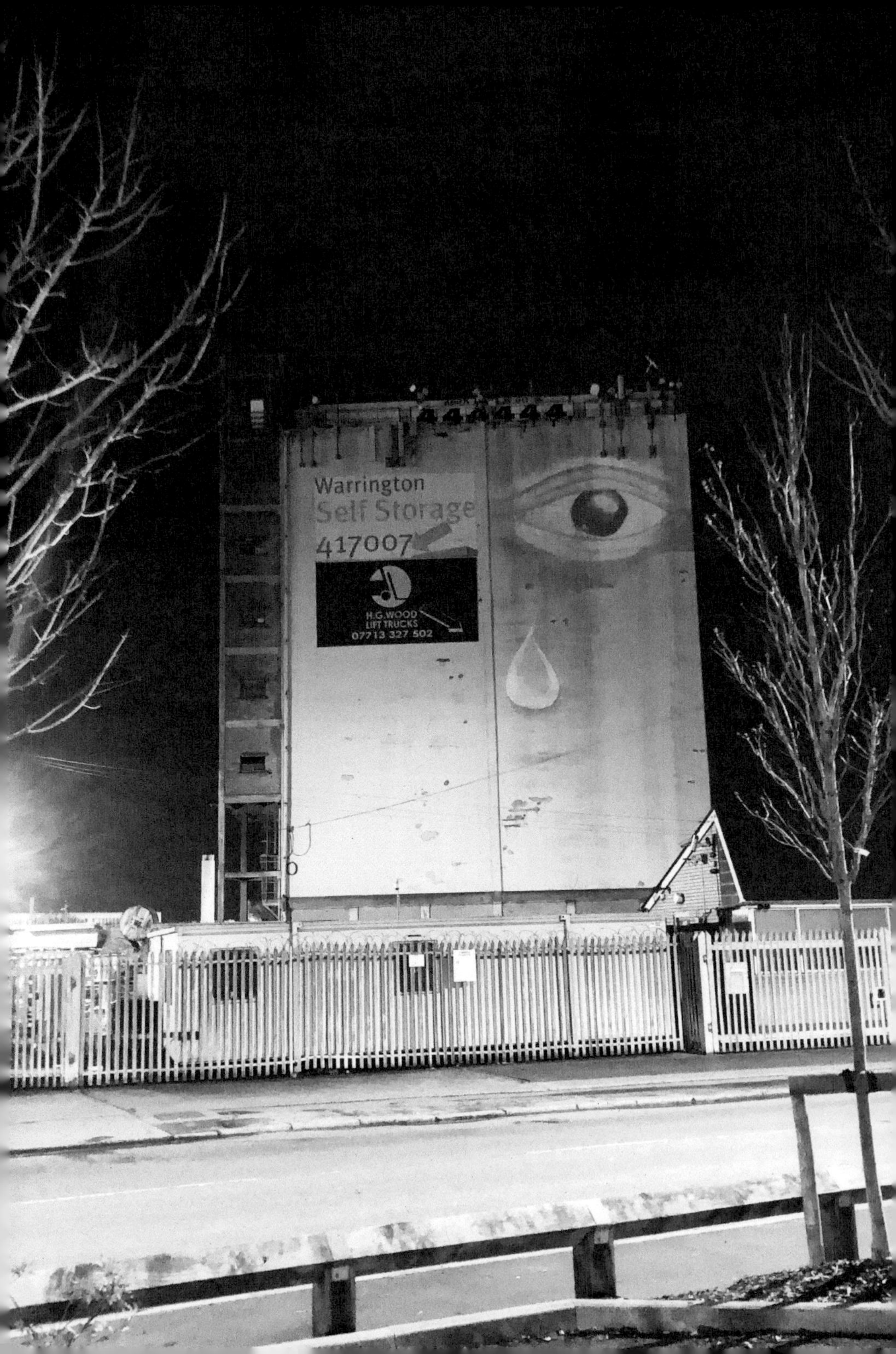
Warrington
Self Storage
417007
H.G.WOOD
LIFT TRUCKS
07713 327 502

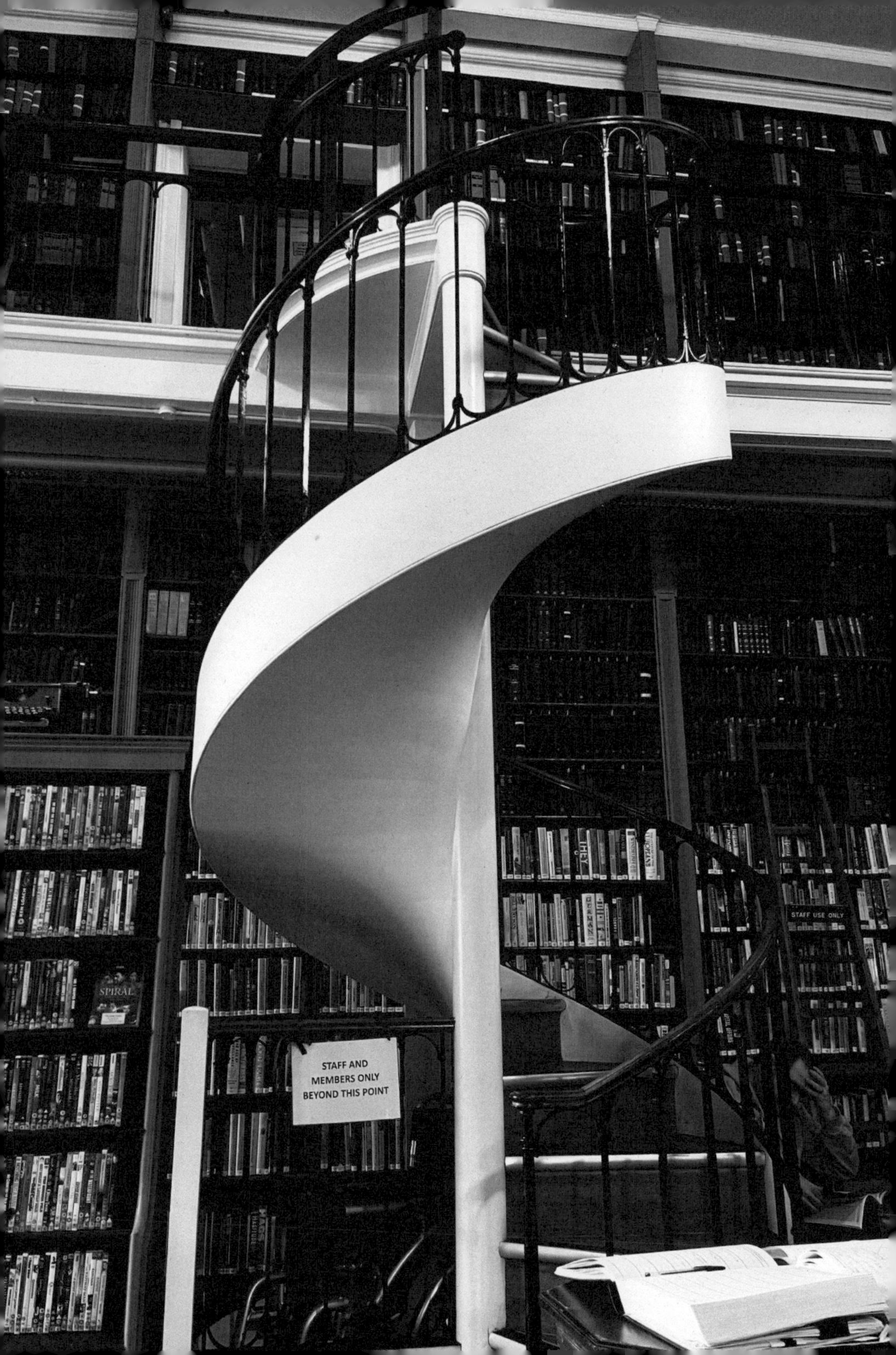
STAFF AND
MEMBERS ONLY
BEYOND THIS POINT
STAFF USE ONLY
SPIRAL

Contributors : Words

Susan Darlington's poetry regularly explores the female experience through nature-based symbolism and stories of transformation. It has been published in Northern Gravy, Dreich, Dream Catcher, Ink Sweat & Tears, and Hedgehog Press among others. Her latest pamphlet is 'Never Wear White' (Alien Buddha Press, 2022). X: @S_sanDarlington

Esta Innes-Limbachia rediscovered her love of poetry as a way of dealing with PTSD and post-natal depression. Her poetry explores motherhood, mental health, and the questions nature can invoke. She has been published in the inaugural Sisterhood anthology and its sequel this Summer, as well as the 2024 York literary review. She also performs around West Yorkshire. Instagram: @eilpoetry

Ezekiel (Zero) Foster-Eardley is a multi-disciplinary artist who has operated in Leeds since 2018. Their poetry is often melancholic and somewhat grandiose as it straddles the line between pithy lamenting and verbose fable, largely touching on existentialism and identity.

Angela Marshall is a working-class poet from the North East of England. Her writing tends to be raw and relating to real life situations. It is her coping mechanism.

Linda Downs is a Northern poet born and raised in Manchester who shares her work on open Mic around Greater Manchester.

Tim Fletcher has written poems since the age of about 14. He plays ukulele, has an allotment and loves social history. He has lived in Southport for 42 years. He is a Northerner and proud to be.

Helen Rice is a writer and performer living in Sheffield. She writes about her experiences as a middle-aged disabled woman and stepmum. Her debut pamphlet, 'I'm Not Your Mother', was published by Written Off in 2024.

Alice Eaves is an artist and writer from Blackpool, whose interest lies in the relationship between ecology, folklore & sexuality. She has been published with The Alchemy Spoon, The Lit Platform & Moonflake Press, and is a Melbourne UNESCO City of Literature virtual writer-in-residence and editor of Tiny Flames (Forest Publishing).

Charles Heathcote has always lived in Macclesfield and very rarely leaves. The author of the Our Doris series of comedic novels, his poetry has previously appeared in Butcher's Dog and The Greenhouse magazine. In 2023, he released his first poetry collection, Shepherd's Delight.

Em MacKellar is a teacher and a poet from Newcastle-upon-Tyne. Surrounded by the Northumberland countryside and the north east coast, Em's poetry focuses entirely on nature and the way that we can use nature to understand ourselves.

Natalie Hurt is an English teacher from Sheffield, where she still lives and works. She grew up working class and was the first person in her family to go to university. The poems she writes are inspired by her life growing up, her transition into adulthood, and she is always inspired by the work she does and the books she teaches.

Candi Martin is a tutor and writer from Lancashire. She has always written for her own wellbeing and writes on nature, social mobility and our roots in this world. She can usually be found listening to Radio 6 music with her two cats. Find her on IG: @candi_says_ @writingforwellnessrossendale

Alan Parry is a writer and editor influenced by 1950's jazz clubs and the social realism of mid-twentieth-century Britain. His work seeks to blend these inspirations into texts that capture the working-class life, in the North of England employing vivid imagery and an imaginative use of language and form.

DH Holmes is a Halifax lad, born along England's greenest hills. Mostly, he writes to cling to the boyish elixir of clothes smeared in vandal grease; bikes robbed from under the kitchen window; and Mum on the doorstep shouting his name. Find him as @about.which on Instagram.

Rebecca Riddell is a content writer by day, and a poet by early evening. Born in Wakefield, she can usually be found writing feminist, queer, and working-class poetry. They are published in a handful of anthologies, and are currently working on their first poetry collection (scary). Follow her on IG: @r.a.riddell.

Emily Mather is a tentative poet and textbook Libra from rainy Manchester. 'Pleasure Beach, You Have the Worst of Me' is about how annual pilgrimages to Blackpool put growing up and growing apart into perspective.

Chris Cottom's flash fiction has been published by Apricot Press, Cosmic Daffodil, Defuncted, Ellipsis Zine, Flash 500, Free Flash Fiction, Hysteria, Leicester Writes, LoveReading, NFFD NZ, NFFD UK, On The Premises, Oxford Flash Fiction, Retreat West, Shooter Flash, The Centifictionist, The Hooghly Review, The Phare, The Storms, Witcraft, and others.

Elizabeth Gibson is a queer, neurodivergent Manchester poet who has been the recipient of a New North Poets Prize from the Poetry School and a DYCP grant from Arts Council England. Poems have appeared in Butcher's Dog, Confingo, Ey Up Again, Lighthouse, Magma, The North, Popshot, and Under the Radar.
https://elizabeth-gibson.com // @Grizonne

Edward Heathman grew up in South Wales and studied English Literature and Creative Writing at the University of Manchester. He has had writing published in The Manchester Anthology, The Visual Verse Anthology and on Ink, Sweat & Tears. He is currently working on a poetry pamphlet centred around sleep disorders.

Karan Heppell has appeared in Red Herring, a Northern pamphlet and was shortlisted in the Hexham Poetry Competition 2023. She will feature in an anthology by LateBritainPress later this year.

Karan writes about her experiences with cancer, her subsequent health problems and the beautiful county she loves.

Carole Thirlaway writes poetry which is often emotionally connected to herself or her life. She is 79 and finds she is often being challenged by a society that seems to see (or not see) older people as being past any useful purpose! She finds poetry helps.

Margaret Montgomery was born and brought up in Wallsend. She lives in Newcastle. She likes factual and political commentary poetry drawn from her experiences. She is unpublished but is keen to know if people relate to her writing.

Rebecca Wright is a poet from West Yorkshire, currently studying English Literature at Newcastle University. Her work usually involves themes of nostalgia, memory, grief, identity and the places where these overlap.

Rob Wheeldon is a writer who also happens to be dyslexic: "I write with the aid of assistive technology and attend Joy Winkler's creative writing classes in Macclesfield most weeks."

GP Hyde studied fine art at Goldsmith's and at the Royal Academy Schools. He has published a pamphlet, 'A Gracious Month', and his short fiction has been extensively published by Pure Slush. His poetry has been published by Black Bough Press, Hedgehog Poetry Press and Bent Key Publishing.

Holly Baron-Morgan is a writer of fiction. She was born and brought up in Warrington and now resides in Bollington on the edge of the Peak District with her husband and two young children. She is currently working on her first novel set in Liverpool, Canada, Alaska and Norway.

J E Neary is an artist and facilitator who writes poetry and narrative non-fiction, primarily around parenthood, grief and longing for home. In 2022 she won the Metro Prize by the Poetry Book Society, and was awarded the Terry Kelly Poetry Prize.

Kai Cohen (he/they) is a Queer Crip who lives with chronic pain and fatigue. He frequently battles with what it means to be working class and poor while all of the above. He writes poems about bereavement, parenting, love, and death. He has three kids and a large dog.

Susan Berry is passionate about creative writing and poetry. She loves to read it, and loves to write it. She also loves animals, particularly dogs, green spaces, and theatre.

Zoe Gardiner is an autistic mother of two, a research scientist, a doula and birth advocate based in County Durham. She writes poems to understand the feelings and the thoughts in her head and body and to make sense of the world as I experience it.

Dawn Rhodes-Shaw is a poet and screenwriter from Leeds, West Yorkshire. She writes primarily about relationships, love, grief, family, and the natural world. Her poems are published online with Underbelly Press, Words and Whispers Journal and Neologism Poetry Journal. She recently won the Sussex Poetry Prize sponsored by New Writing South.

Daniel Findell is a poet from Liverpool. He has had work published in literary journals internationally and won the inaugural Literary Lancashire Award for Poetry in 2019. Following completion of Creative Writing MA at Lancaster University in 2022 he now resides in Manchester, where he can be found performing at poetry nights across the city and beyond.

Elliot Chester is an avid writer and reader. He's written on many themes, loves to write on train journeys and has a fascination with the cosmos, the darkness, and all things mystical. He has self-published his own rhyme and colouring book and is working towards official publication.

Vella H is 22 years old and an aspiring writer. She is a bisexual woman who loves to write about difficult relationships and substance abuse but also about how magical life can be.

Amy B Garratt is a Spoken Word Performer, Poet, MA Student and BA Graduate, yet still doesn't have a 'proper career'. She indie-published a collection in 2021: 'Sunlight Stripping Shadows Bare' which was written during the 2020 lockdowns about depression/moving forward. She has been previously published in the 'Ey Up Again' Anthology, Dreich Magazine, and HNDL Magazine.

Beck Alexander was born and raised in Manchester and is currently a 2nd year English and Creative Writing student at MMU. He is a prose and script writer, and his work revolves around both middle and working-class realism. He cites Raymond Carver as a literary inspiration.

Chris Barras is a poet living in Whitehaven, Cumbria. His poetry is written with minimal capitalisation and punctuation to allow the words to speak for themselves. His work is influenced by life in Cumbria and the sea viewed from his back window.

Anne-Marie Draycott is a writer, actor, coach, mum, walker, yoga-lover & occasional forager.

Anna Brizzolara lives in Knaresborough, North Yorkshire and is a single parent currently studying for a Creative Writing MA at York St John University. Her work intimately dissects marriage, examining shame and control through the lens of domesticity.

Lorna Rose Gill is a poet and founder of the Orange Verse. She comes from many places, but lives on the Wirral with a lovely man and two dogs. She writes about what it means to be a woman living right here, right now, in this place.

Lewis Brown is a Newcastle-based writer and founder of the Spooky Poet Club. He prefers to write platonic love poems, but sometimes he wakes up in an abandoned building surrounded by tattered pages of horror poetry which are in his handwriting, but which he has no memory of writing.

Mymona Bibi is a writer and ESOL teacher based in Newcastle. Her writing has been featured in the Ilkley Literature Festival and Lumpen Press and explores topics of identity and trauma. Currently, she is interested in writing about homes within the context of a social housing crisis in the UK.

Vanessa Napolitano is from Yorkshire and is a dual British-American citizen. Her poetry has been published lately in Poetry Wales, and Stanchion Zine, and her first chapbook is due out this year with Black Cat Poetry Press. She writes about place, nature, grief and motherhood.

Owen Townend is a writer of short speculative fiction and poetry inspired by thought experiment and wordplay. His work is published in anthologies from Comma Press, Maytree Press, Oxford Spires Publishing and others. He lives in Huddersfield, West Yorkshire and is a member of the Huddersfield Authors' Circle.

Rosa Wright is a poet, performer and professional weirdo. She is the editor of Swordplay Zine and lead singer for Illegal Fireworks.

Eleanor May Blackburn is a 27 year-old queer, neurodivergent, disabled actor/writer from Sheffield. She had a Chapbook 'Ghost and Found' published by Cerasus Poetry in 2021 has been published in Full House, Southchild Lit and Glitchwords amongst others. She writes about trauma and feminist narratives, predominantly through comedy.

E.M. Davis is a poet/musician living by the North-East coast. Her poetry centres on post-natal depression, OCD, love, loss and the definition of the self. Poems have been featured in the Kaleidoscopic Minds anthology, The Winged Moon, The Wee Sparrow Poetry Press and Motherlore Magazine. Online she's found @ifgoldrusts

Joy Winkler is a poet who is author of several collections. She's a former Cheshire Poet Laureate and has written and performed her own verse/drama as well as a play called 'Lightning under their

Skirts'. She is Writer in Residence at RHS Tatton Park where she delivers creative writing workshops.

Eleanor Dickinson was born in West Yorkshire, lives on the Lancashire/Manchester Border and is in her forties.

Fee Marshall is an autistic trans poet and all that jazz. Their art entails talking to cats, childhood memories, and platonic love letters.

Grace Copeland, 24, is a Creative Writing Masters student at the University of Oxford. She works in prison education with men who have learning difficulties and complex mental health. Grace is working on her first collection, which explores the lyricism of life in the North East, centring her relationship with Sunderland, her hometown.

Jen Corcoran describes herself as Northern, Feminist and Socialist. She enjoys writing that intrigues, celebrates and informs. Her debut collection, Witch/Mother/Child/Lover was published by Written Off Publishing in 2023.

Hilary Elder (she/her) was born, raised and lives in the Far North of England – though she has been to other places. She writes fiction and poetry for children and adults, short fiction, creative non-fiction and sermons, published including in Northern Gravy, Tyger Tyger and The Caterpillar. www.hilaryelder.com // @hilaryelderwrites

James Jackson is a Manchester-based poet and writer. Dealing with themes of esotericism, alchemy, occultism, nature and folklore, James weaves narratives with layered metaphors that create a tapestry of meaning. Each listener finds their own meaning within the work.

Grace Ward is 38 years old and currently living in Castlefield which is surprisingly a quieter end of town. She has lived in Manchester all her life, growing up in the north of the city (Blackley). She mainly writes poems, the occasional short story and has nearly finished a very messy first draft of a novel; all these, she does whilst working full time. Writing is her saviour and helps her make sense of this crazy life.

Gary Bunting is a Yorkshire postman and has recently been featured in Ey Up Again, Mantis and The Nuthatch. He also records audio versions of his poems for the Hello America Stereo Cassette record label.

Kate Hook is a cheese enthusiast, mum, writer and poet. Her debut collection of poetry, I Can Hear You Ironing, was published in 2023 by Brown Dog Books.

Ilisha Thiru Purcell is an award winning poet from Newcastle whose work explores place, liminality, and violence. She is part of the Poets of Colour Incubator, a previous Young Creative Associate with New Writing North, and performed at the Newcastle Poetry Festival. Her work has appeared in Butcher's Dog, Bi+ Lines Anthology, and was shortlisted for Primers Vol.7.

Brigid Griffin is from Macclesfield. She now lives in Northumberland. Her writing is inspired by Northern communities, personal experiences, animals, people and relationships. She has been published in Written Off Publishing's 2023 'Ey Up Again' Anthology and was placed third in 2023's Story Tyne competition. She has had articles published in Write on! magazine and her novel When the Small Creatures Wake is being published in November 2024 by Write on the Tyne.

Andrew Mears is a retired retail manager who is now fully absorbed in creative writing. He has published two poetry collections and facilitates a number of local writing groups to allow writers of any experience to flourish and maximise their potential.

Charlie Parker is a writer and political activist based in Sheffield. His debut collection, 'It's Like This.' was published in 2023 by Written Off Publishing, and has been nominated for multiple wards. He has performed across the UK and once in Europe. He is currently writing a novella.

Moya Ozyer-Key is a twenty-two year-old creative writing student and an intense lover of surrealism and defamiliarization. Her piece is inspired by a shopping trip to Tesco to retrieve ground beef and strawberry laces for a lasagne that she subsequently dropped all over the floor.

Natalie Cooper is a poet, writer and performer based in Leeds, who writes about family, belonging, growing up and finding a place in the world. Their poems are typically written to be performed aloud, and focus on personal topics.

Sarah Cain is a teaching assistant and mum of four from Harrogate, North Yorkshire. She has a strong passion for science poetry and has recently been exploring our place in the universe. Her work has been published in a number of anthologies and zines including York Literary Review (2022).

Charlotte Walker is a writer, reader and yoga teacher living in Liverpool. She writes poetry, and is interested in moments of everyday life that could easily escape our notice, but which seem to call us towards something bigger than ourselves. Pausing and listening to these moments is often where her poems begin.

Amy Frances is a fair-to-middling poet from Bradford in West Yorkshire, where she lives and writes. She writes poems about nature and feelings and off-season seaside towns, mostly. She likes playing around with different poetic forms, partly for the joy of it, and partly because whittling words down to fit into a form makes it seem a little easier to write.

Lyndsey Dickinson is a teacher and currently works with international students. Her creative work mainly consists of short stories and poems, and she is keen to pursue other writing styles. She has a keen interest in all things language and believes everyone should have access to linguistic expression.

Barbara Callaghan is originally from Liverpool, but has lived in York for 20 years. She is a mum and nan who loves words and tries to write poetry for fun.

Andrew James Murray is a writer and poet who still lives in his hometown of Middleton, Manchester. His short fiction has appeared in various anthologies, and he has had three poetry collections published: Heading North, In Brigantia, and Fifty. His work has featured in Best Of Manchester Poets. He can be found at cityjackdaw.wordpress.com

Dan Hughes is a content writer by day and a scribbler of oddball prose by night. Some of the work features in lit magazines, print anthologies, and on the radio. He splits his time between Cheshire and Co. Durham. He also loves HobNobs.

Helen Aitchison is an author from North East England. Published three times with Cahill Davis Publishing, Helen has also featured in a number of anthologies. She is director of Write on the Tyne CIC, a non-profit aiming to make creative writing inclusive and accessible.

Joanna Kay is a writer, artist, creative workshop facilitator and therapist. She loves to write poems and fiction on spirituality, identity, travel, love, relationships and family dynamics.

Lexus Luke-Walsh is a 20 year-old BA(Hons) English student who tutors on the side. She has written a piece of poetry that explained all the opinions and controversies of being a woman and how we feel in the modern world trying to fight for the things we shouldn't have to fight for.

Ellie Spirrett is a poet and spoken word performer. She was the 2023 Some-Antics slam champion and a 2023 Roundhouse slam finalist. Her work has been published in Flight of the Dragonfly and Barzakh Magazine. She writes about chronic illness, ableism, the cost of living and the loneliness pandemic.

Karen Kendrick is a writer and creative writing teacher. She writes poetry and prose. She is from a working-class background and this influences a lot of her writing, although she likes to write about a wide range of things. She is currently working on a set of poems about the 'bad girls' of fiction (because they are often the most interesting characters). You can find her online: https://peculiarthings.blog/

Julia Ellis is a mature student in her final year studying English Language, Literature and Creative Writing at the Blackpool & Fylde College University Centre in Blackpool. Her art submission is a poetic ballad that she wrote as part of her first-year creative writing portfolio.

Contributors : Images

Rebecca Kenny is the founder of Written Off Publishing. She usually writes poetry, but for Ey Up 3, she's submitted photos instead.

Debbie Wingell is a multi-media artist who uses nature-inspired drawing, writing & photography to help manage her mental health. Having recently recognised that she is autistic, she continues to explore art as a way to gain understanding of her personal experience and the world around her.

Hannah Dixon, born in Warrington, loves the town very much as well as adventures growing in Manchester, Cumbria, the Lake District, West Yorkshire and round abouts. She is interested in word-building and photo creations with heart for beloved mates, mental health, memory and happiness.

Beckett Kenny is only six years old, but he likes taking photos. Perhaps one day he will do it for a living.

Harry Poyzer is from Nottingham, but has lived in Leeds for four years.

Rosa Wright also has a poem in this collection. You will have already read her bio on page 134.

Lauren Chadwick is a proudly Northern bookseller and emerging writer and poet who thinks poetry is for everyone and should be widely accessible. She writes a lot about family, grief, social class, (all the light-hearted stuff), and finding her place as a second-generation immigrant, working-class woman in a world that doesn't cater too much for that.

McKenzie Duncan is currently in their third year at LAU studying creative writing where they focus on themes of identity, family dynamics and culture (in the form of poetry, prose or narrative essays). They've found memoir writing to be their calling.

Alex Callaghan is a poet and the editor of Ey Up 3. They also run Bone Down, a poetry event in Leeds that aims to reclaim space for art.

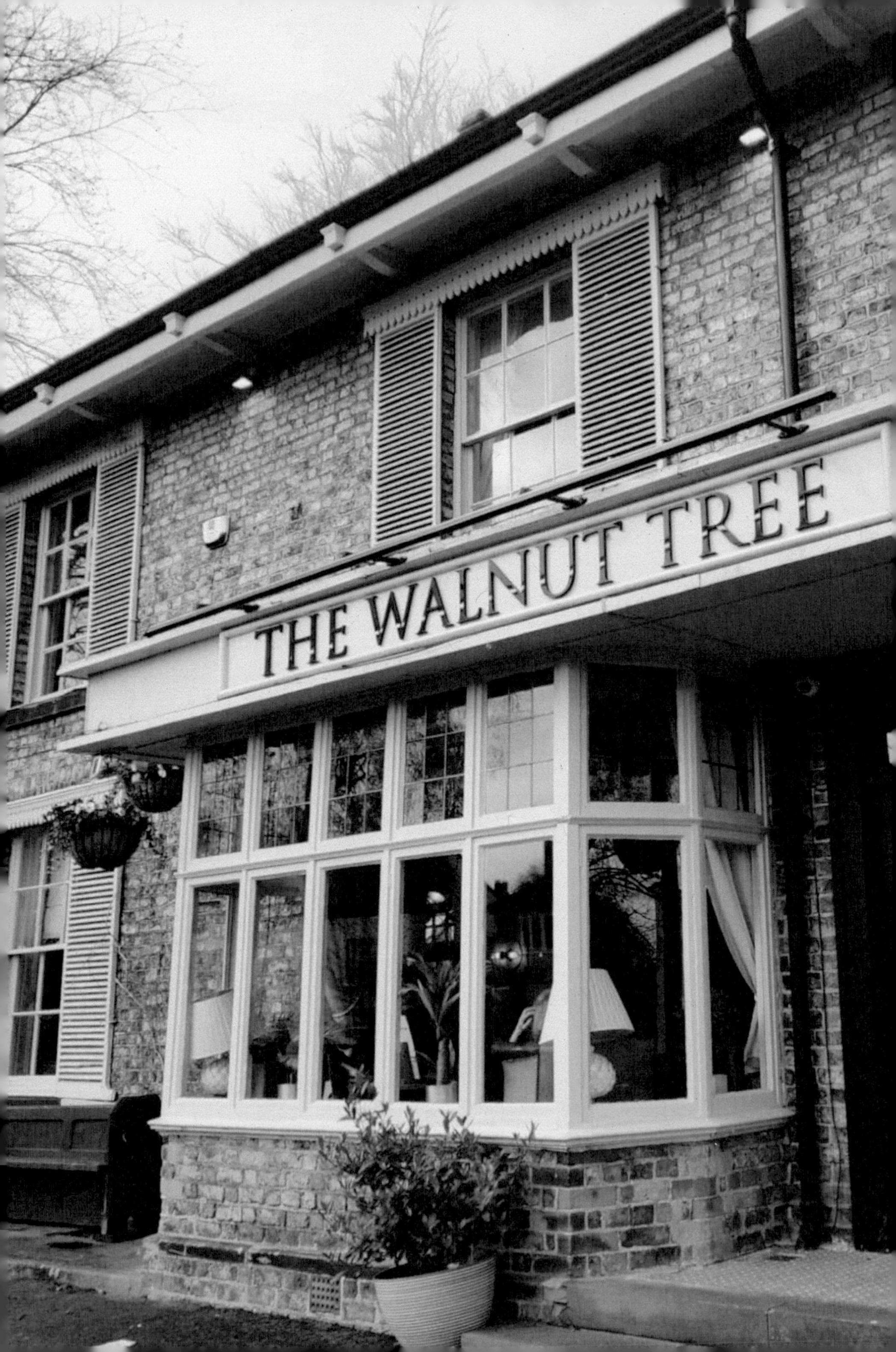
THE WALNUT TREE

Images

Page 1
View from atop The Anderton Boat Lift, *Cheshire* : Rebecca Kenny

Page 2
Phone box, *Cheshire* : Hannah Dixon

Page 5
Malham View, *North Yorkshire* : Debbie Wingell

Page 6
Lancastrian Hall, *Greater Manchester* : Lauren Chadwick

Page 7
Trees in Sefton Park, *Merseyside* : Beckett Kenny

Page 8
Dinos in Golden Acre Park, *West Yorkshire* : Harry Poyzer

Page 12
View from Knaresborough Castle, *North Yorkshire* : Harry Poyzer

Page 16
Leeds Market, *West Yorkshire* : Rosa Wright

Page 48
Railway Crossing, *West Yorkshire* : Harry Poyzer

Page 90
Abandoned Sofa in Owley Wood, *Cheshire* : Rebecca Kenny

Page 126
The Pink Eye, Cheshire : Hannah Dixon

Page 127
Leeds Library spiral staircase, *West Yorkshire* : McKenzie Duncan

Page 142
The Walnut Tree, *West Yorkshire* : Alex Callaghan

About The Publisher

Written Off is a publishing company founded in and run from the North of England. It came into existence after Founder Rebecca Kenny's arrival home from hospital following a car crash in which she broke her neck, back, pelvis, sternum and sacrum. Its logo, an open umbrella, acts as a symbol of change, new starts, risk and taking a chance on the unknown.

Having her car written off, her career written off, and then being somewhat written off herself, Rebecca chose the company's name with an aim to reclaim power from adversity and show that just because society maintains a status quo, that doesn't mean you can't make waves.

Written Off do not charge for submissions, we do not charge to publish and we make space for writers who may struggle to access traditional publishing houses, specifically writers who are neuro-divergent or otherwise marginalised. We never ask anyone to centre their trauma, and we like to champion authentic voices.

All of our beautiful covers are designed by independent queer artists. Please do take the time to follow their work.

Find us online at writtenoffpublishing.com